I Love New York Cooking from Other Lands.

The American Cancer Society
New York State Division, Inc.

DEDICATION

1982 "I Love New York Cooking From Other Lands" is dedicated to all the New York State Division, Inc. Volunteers who are helping to find the greatest recipe of all—the Cure for Cancer.

First Printing, Limited Edition   25,000   1981
International Standard Book Number—0-939114-15-1

Printed in the United States of America
Wimmer Brothers Fine Printing & Lithography
Memphis, Tennessee 38118
"Cookbooks of Distinction"™

IN APPRECIATION

"I Love New York Cooking From Other Lands," 1982 Edition has been published as a fund-raising project for the New York State Division of the American Cancer Society.

It is the intent of the Volunteers and Staff of the New York State Division to publish a series of these Cookbooks on an annual basis so that home-makers will have a set for their kitchens. It is also intended that said series will become a collector's set for those who collect cookbooks and favorite recipes. We sincerely hope that you will take great pride in having this book and will enjoy using the favorite recipes and will look forward to the succeeding editions.

The next cookbook in this series will be "I Love New York Holiday Cooking."

This book is the product of the efforts of many dedicated Volunteers who were kind enough to share their favorite recipes.

We wish to express our deepest appreciation for the editing of the cookbook to:

Professor Matteo A. Casola, Chairman
Department of Hotel Technology
Schenectady Community College
Schenectady, New York 12305

An especial thanks to Executive Chef, Pasquale "Pat" Rocco, Restaurant and Chef's Consultant and Chairman of "I Love New York Cooking from Other Lands."

TABLE OF CONTENTS

Appetizers

JOHNNY APPLESEED

John Chapman, more commonly known as Johnny Appleseed, was of Swedish descent. The legend tells us that on a bright sunny morning when Johnny Appleseed was 18 years of age, he slung a knapsack on his back and set out to see for himself the rich land that lay beyond the Applachians. His destination was a speck on the map that would in time become the town of Olean. There, lived a relative known to the family as Uncle Ben. Using the stars as a compass and shadowy Indian trails for a path he trudges northward.

By the time he reached Olean the autumn leaves were falling and Uncle Ben offered to put him up for the winter in return for help with the chores.

His first opportunity came when he heard of a nearby farmer who owned a cider mill. Johnny searched him out and asked if he might have the hard drums of crusted, decaying pomace, which when carefully washed and sifted yielded a quart of seeds. On a marshy spot near Olean he sowed them in rows and grew his first orchard. From then on Johnny worked his way westward until the Central and Northern part of Ohio was dotted with orchards. He was accustomed to clearing a place in the forest; planting his appleseeds; fencing in the patch and when the locality was settled asking payment of either a "flip-penny bit" per tree, clothes or food, although frequently he gave them away.

He went unarmed and was never molested by the Indians or wild beasts. The Indians regarded him as a great "medicine man", because he scattered seeds of medicinal plants, such as catnip and pennyroyal throughout the woods. He mainly wore an old coffee sack with holes for his head and arms and carried a tin pot which he used to cook in and sometimes donned as a hat.

STUFFED CELERY
French

1 tablespoon Roquefort cheese	1 pinch salt
4 tablespoons cream cheese	Paprika
1 tablespoon butter	Celery stalks

Combine Roquefort cheese with cream cheese, butter and salt. Stuff celery stalks and sprinkle with paprika to taste.

Volunteer
Lewis County

STUFFED MUSHROOMS PARMIGIANA
Italian

12 large mushrooms	3 tablespoons Parmesan
2 tablespoons butter	cheese, grated
1 medium onion, finely chopped	1 tablespoon parsley, snipped
½ cup (2 ounces) pepperoni, diced	½ teaspoon seasoned salt
¼ cup green pepper, finely chopped	¼ teaspoon dried oregano, crushed
1 small clove garlic, minced	Dash pepper
½ cup (12 crackers) rich round crackers, finely crushed	⅓ cup chicken broth

Wash mushrooms. Remove and finely chop stems. Drain caps on paper toweling. Melt butter in skillet add onions, pepperoni, green pepper, garlic and chopped mushroom stems. Cook until vegetables are tender but not brown. Add cracker crumbs, cheese, parsley, seasoned salt, oregano and pepper. Mix well. Stir in chicken broth. Spoon stuffing into mushroom caps, rounding tops. Place caps in shallow baking pan with about ¼-inch of water covering bottom of pan. Bake, uncovered in 325 degree oven about 25 minutes or until heated through.

Bridget Colella
Cayuga County

MUSHROOMS BOURGUIGNON
French

1 pound large mushroom caps
2 cloves garlic, crushed
⅓ cup butter
1 cup burgundy

1 small green onion, chopped
1 teaspoon parsley, chopped
1 pinch black pepper
Toast rounds

Add garlic, onion, parsley and pepper to burgundy. Place in saucepan over high heat and reduce mixture to one half original volume. Allow to cool, then cream with butter. Sauté mushroom caps in butter, then place on toast rounds. Top with burgundy mixture.

Volunteer
Chenango County

CAPONATO
(Eggplant Relish)
Italian

1 medium to large eggplant, unpeeled (cut in ½-inch cubes)
1 large yellow onion, chopped
1 large green pepper, seeded and chopped
2 medium ripe tomatoes, chopped
2 ribs celery, chopped
1 cup fresh mushrooms, sliced
⅓ cup pimiento-stuffed green olives, cut in half

4 cloves garlic, finely minced
½ cup olive oil
⅓ cup red wine vinegar
1 tablespoon salt
3 tablespoons sugar
¼ teaspoon ground pepper
½ teaspoon dried oregano
½ teaspoon dried basil
1 tablespoon capers

In a large pot combine all the ingredients, mixing thoroughly. Cook over low heat, uncovered for about one hour, stirring occasionally, until the mixture is soft and all the liquid has cooked away. Cool, then refrigerate. Serves 6-8. Freezes well.

Note: Serve as an appetizer, relish, or spread. It will keep for several weeks in refrigerator. It can be eaten chilled or at room temperature.

Theresa Paulus
Ulster County

FRIED EGGPLANT STICKS
Greek

1 medium eggplant
¾ cup flour
½ teaspoon salt

¼ cup olive oil
¼ cup vegetable shortening

Peel eggplant. Cut into lengthwise strips ¼ inch thick, 1 inch wide, and 3-4 inches long. Generously sprinkle both sides with salt. Put strips in a colander. Weight them down with several plates. Allow bitter juices to drain out for an hour. Roll strips in combined flour and salt. Heat oil and shortening together. Fry strips over medium-high heat until crispy and golden brown. Drain on paper towels. Arrange around a bowl of Creamy Garlic Dip. Use forks to dip sticks in sauce.

Volunteer
Allegany County

CREAMY GARLIC DIP
Greek

3 medium potatoes (1½ cups, mashed)
6-8 garlic cloves
¼ cup olive oil

1 tablespoon fresh lemon juice
1½ teaspoons salt
2 dashes pepper
¼ cup chicken broth

Peel, quarter and boil potatoes in unsalted water. Drain and mash. Peel garlic. Press or mince finely. Place in large bowl. Mash into a juicy pulp with bottom of teaspoon. Add mashed potatoes. Blend with a fork. Beat in oil, a few teaspoons at a time, until completely absorbed by potatoes. Mix in lemon juice, salt and pepper. Add chicken broth, a little at a time. Continue blending to a smooth, creamy consistency. Serve at room temperature with fried eggplant sticks. Makes almost 2 cups.

Volunteer
Allegany County

BLACK OLIVES
Greek

2 pounds small, pointed black Greek olives	2 lemons, thinly sliced
Vinegar to cover	Celery stalks, coarsely chopped
	Olive oil

Crack the olives with a hammer until the pits show and cover them with the vinegar. Let stand two days. Drain and pack into sterilized jars, arranging the olives alternately with layers of lemon slices and celery. Cover with olive oil and keep in a cool place until ready to serve. Serves 12-18.

Volunteer
Rensselaer County

MARINATED PORK STRIPS
Korean

2 pork tenderloins	2 cloves garlic, minced
½ cup soy sauce	2 teaspoons ground ginger
3 tablespoons sugar	¾ cup sesame seeds
2 tablespoons onions, minced	2 tablespoons oil

Preheat oven to moderate 375 degrees. Trim the fat from the tenderloins. If thick, split lengthwise. Combine the remaining ingredients except the oil in a bowl. Marinate the pork in the mixture 3 hours in the refrigerator, turning and basting frequently. Drain and reserve the marinade. Transfer the pork to an oiled roasting pan and roast until tender, about 45 minutes. Simmer the marinade 10 minutes. Cut the pork into thin slices and serve on cocktail picks with the marinade as an hors d'oeuvre. Serves 16.

Volunteer
Rensselaer County

KOREAN CHICKEN
Korean

6-8 chicken wings
½ cup water
½ cup soy sauce
2 cloves garlic, finely chopped

3 scallions, chopped, using
  whole stalk
1 teaspoon sugar

Cut off and discard tip of wing. Cut through the joint in wing. Add a small amount of water to a skillet and sauté briefly on each side. Add soy sauce, water, garlic and scallions. Sprinkle with the sugar. Arrange chicken wings in a single layer in the pan. Cover and simmer slowly, turning once. Add more water if necessary. Cook approximately 45 minutes, or until tender and browned.

Mrs. John Cina
Dutchess County

RUMAKI
Oriental

1 pound chicken livers
½ cup soy suace
¼ cup sherry
¼ teaspoon black pepper
1 clove garlic, crushed

2 cans water chestnuts, sliced
¾ pound bacon, each slice cut
  in halves or thirds
Toothpicks

Cut chicken livers in half and trim off any fat. Combine soy sauce, sherry, garlic, and pepper and pour over the livers. Cover and marinate at least one hour. After marinating, preheat oven to 400 degrees. Now wrap half a chicken liver and a slice of water chestnut in a piece of bacon and secure with a toothpick. Set on a rack on a cookie sheet and bake in oven for about 20 minutes. Do not turn. This full recipe makes about 36 appetizers.

Note: I often cut this recipe in half.

Mrs. Marshall Scott
Herkimer County

GE'HOKTE LEIBER
(Chopped Liver)
Jewish

1 pound chicken livers
1 large onion
3 eggs, hard-boiled

2 tablespoons "schmaltz"
(rendered chicken fat or
substitute shortening)
1 teaspoon salt

Broil chicken livers (can be partly broiled and then sautéed to completion with half the onion). When cooled, add the cooled hard-boiled eggs, sliced raw onion (or remainder of onion), chop all ingredients, or run through a grinder, adding the salt and schmaltz gradually.

Note: In my home, when I was a youth, this was usually served as an appetizer for the Sabbath meals. Serve on crackers.

Irwin Gooen
Otsego County

SAÜR KRUV
(Sour Sausage)
Scandinavian

7 pounds potatoes
5 large onions
3½ pounds ground beef (with a
bit of fat in it)
1½ pounds ground pork

3 teaspoons allspice
1 teaspoon black pepper
2 tablespoons salt
1 pound beef or pork casings

Peel potatoes and leave whole. Cook until half done. (Test one by cutting in half.) Cool immediately and cut in half to prevent further cooking. Boil the onions until half done and drain, reserving the liquid. Grind onions and potatoes and add to the beef, pork, allspice, black pepper, and salt. Stuff casings with a sausage stuffer. (The casings come packed in salt, so rinse under cold water. Sometimes the casings are precut to certain lengths, if not they will have to be cut to lengths wanted.) Hang to dry in moderately warm area (68-70 degrees for approximately 4-7 days.) They will be red-dish-brown and shrivelled. Fry in heavy skillet, on low flame, with no grease as they will make their own grease, until brown on both sides, about 15-30 minutes. Cut into bite size pieces.

Suzanne Blanchard
Hamilton County

SHRIMP TOAST
Oriental

10 slices sandwich bread
½ pound deveined cooked
  shrimp, finely chopped
½ pound ground pork
1 small onion, minced
1 teaspoon salt
1 teaspoon granulated sugar

¼ teaspoon monosodium
  glutamate
1 tablespoon cornstarch
2 eggs, lightly beaten
Fine dry bread crumbs
2 cups cooking oil

Trim the crusts from the bread. Mix shrimp, pork, onion, salt, sugar, mono-sodium glutamate, and cornstarch. Add eggs and mix together well. Spread mixture over the bread and cover with the bread crumbs, pressing the crumbs into the surface. Gently shake off excess bread crumbs. Cut each slice into four squares or triangles. Heat cooking oil to 375 degrees. Sauté the bread, shrimp side down, until golden brown. Turn and cook the other side. Drain on absorbent paper. Serves 8.

Min H. Theresa Chang
Cortland County

HOT CRAB CANAPÉS AKVAVIT
Scandinavian

½ pound fresh, frozen or
  canned crabmeat (drained
  and picked)
1 tablespoon sherry
1 teaspoon salt
⅛ teaspoon white pepper

1 tablespoon fresh dill, chopped
1 tablespoon butter
1 tablespoon flour
1 egg yolk
1 cup light cream
6 slices white bread

Combine the crabmeat, sherry, salt, pepper and dill. Melt butter and stir in the flour. Beat the egg yolk with the cream and stir mixtures into the butter-flour roux. Cook slowly, whisking constantly for a minute or two until the mixture thickens, do not let boil. Pour sauce over the crabmeat mixture and stir to combine ingredients. Serve on toasted bread rounds. Yields: 24.

Mrs. Peter Geitner
Oswego County

HOT CRABMEAT PUFFS
Scandinavian

1 stick butter or margarine
1 jar Kraft Old English cheese
  (5 ounces)
1½ teaspoons mayonnaise

½ teaspoon seasoned salt
1 6½-ounce can crabmeat
6 English muffins

First soften margarine or butter, then add to cheese in a medium mixing bowl. Stir in mayonnaise and seasoned salt. Drain crabmeat mixture and remove cartilage and break it into chunks. Gently fold into cheese mixture. Split English muffins in half and cut into bite size pieces. Spread crab mixture onto English muffins, placing them on a cookie sheet. Freeze pieces for ten minutes then broil until golden brown or cheese is bubbly, 3-5 minutes. English muffins may be slightly toasted for a crunchier appetizer. These also may be stored frozen to be used at a later date by putting in a plastic bag after freezing on a cookie sheet. Serves 10-12.

Note: This recipe can be doubled.

Maxine R. Flagg
Tioga County

ROQUEFORT PUFFS
French

2 ounces roquefort spread
1 egg white

Paprika to taste
8 small toast rounds

Beat egg whites until stiff, then fold into cheese, heap generously on toast rounds. Place in slow oven about 15 minutes until brown. Sprinkle with paprika to taste.

Volunteer
Schuyler County

SCORDALIA
(Score-dahl-*yah*)
Greek

2 large potatoes
8 cloves garlic
1 tablespoon salt

¼ cup vinegar
1½ cups olive oil
½ cup milk

Peel, dice and boil potatoes. Mash thoroughly while hot. (Try to get rid of lumps.) In a separate mixer bowl, crush garlic well and rub with salt into paste. Add ⅛ cup of the vinegar and ¼ cup of the oil. Beat in mashed potatoes. Gradually add milk and remaining oil and vinegar. Use quantities given as guidelines, not a rigid rule. The dip should be creamy but not runny.

Garlic dip for bread. Scordalia is also delicious served atop sliced cooked beets or on slices of eggplant (aubergine) or zucchini squash (courgettes) which have been dipped in flour and fried.

Peggy Platonos
Yates County

CHILI CON QUESO
(Hot Cheese Dip)
Spanish-Hispanic

2 pounds Velveeta cheese
1 medium onion, chopped
1 16-ounce can tomatoes
2 tablespoons butter

3-4 hot chili peppers (canned, from Mexican section of market)

Melt cheese in double boiler over boiling water. Meanwhile, sauté chopped onion in butter in frying pan. Drain tomatoes and add to onion. Cook until most of moisture has disappeared. Add onion-tomato mixture to melted cheese in double boiler. Cut up chili peppers and add to cheese mixture, seeds and all. Simmer slowly until flavors are blended. Serve in chafing dish over heat with corn chips.

Peg Churchill Wright
Schenectady County

JANSON'S TEMPTATION
Swedish

5 medium potatoes, cut into
  fine strips
2 yellow onions, sliced thin

10 anchovies or 20 anchovy
  fillets
¼ cup butter
1½ cups cream

Preheat oven to moderate 325 degrees. In a buttered baking dish, place a layer of half the potatoes. Add a layer of onions, the anchovies, then the remaining potatoes. Dot with butter and the anchovy juice. Bake 10 minutes. Add half the cream and cook 10 minutes longer. Add the remaining cream and bake 40 minutes longer.

Volunteer
Livingston County

CHEESE BEOREG
Armenian

Dough
1 package sheet dough or
  phyllo dough

Filling
1-pound brick cheese, grated
10-ounces cottage cheese

5 eggs
Parsley, chopped (optional)

Preheat oven to 400 degrees. In large bowl mix grated brick cheese, cottage cheese, eggs and parsley. Cut sheet dough in long strips about 3-4-inches wide. Keep dough covered with damp towel when not handling. Place filling on bottom of narrow side of strip then fold over into a triangle and continue rolling always in a triangle shape. Place filled dough triangles on a buttered baking pan, brush each triangle with melted butter and bake in 400 degree oven until lightly brown. Serve hot.

Note: This can be frozen after preparing. Dough is very brittle when frozen.

Mrs. Deborah Berjouhi Slating
Yates County

DIP IN RYE BREAD
English

1⅓ cups of sour cream
1½ cups of mayonnaise
2 tablespoons of dill weed
2 tablespoons of minced onion

2 tablespoons of parsley
2 3-ounce packages of sliced
  dried beef

Blend sour cream, mayonnaise, dill weed, minced onion, and parsley together. Cut up dried beef into small pieces and add to mixture. Chill mixture until ready to serve. When ready to serve scoop out a loaf of dark rye bread and place the dip in the opening in the bread. Cut the part of the bread that you scooped out into cubes and use for dipping.

Mrs. William Magee
Madison County

MON DOO
Oriental

1 pound hamburg
1 pound pork, ground
1 pound or 1 can beansprouts
  (fresh best)
1 egg
4 cloves of garlic, mashed
2 tablespoons of sesame oil
2 tablespoons soy sauce
1 small piece fresh ginger,
  finely cut

1 pound bean curd, mashed
6 or 7 whole water chestnuts,
  finely cut
½ teaspoon pepper
½ teaspoon MSG (optional)
1 package wonton or Gyoza
  skins
1 egg white, beaten

Mix together: hamburg, ground pork, beansprouts, egg, garlic, sesame oil, soy sauce, ginger, bean curd, water chestnuts, pepper, MSG.

Put egg white around edge of Gyoza skins and place 1 teaspoon of meat mixture in skin. Seal skin securely around edge. Fry at medium heat until golden on both sides. Dip soy sauce, sesame oil and a little rice vinegar mixture. Delicious as an appetizer, with rice or in soup.

Sok Nam & Elaine Ko
Montgomery County

ENGLISH PICKLED EGGS
English

12 hard-boiled eggs, shelled   Beet juice (optional)
Cider vinegar
1 teaspoon mixed pickling
  spices

Pack cooked eggs in jar. Cover with vinegar and a sprinkle of pickling spices. A little beet juice can be added to give them a pink color. Leave in jar 1 month or more. Serve as an appetizer or with cold meats.

Volunteer
Niagara County

CAPONATA
(Sicilian Style)
Italian

2 medium eggplants, peeled,   ¼ cup parsley, chopped
  diced   6 black olives, coarsely
¾ cup olive oil   chopped
2 onions, sliced   ¼ cup red wine vinegar
½ cup tomato puree (not sauce   2 tablespoons sugar
  or paste)   ¼ teaspoon salt
2 stalks celery, diced   ¼ teaspoon pepper
¼ cup capers, drained   ¼ teaspoon dried oregano

Fry eggplant in ½ cup of the olive oil until soft. Remove eggplant and reserve. Add remaining oil to frypan and sauté onion until soft. Add tomato puree, celery and cook until celery is tender. Stir constantly and add a little water if mixture tends to scorch. Add capers, parsley, black olives and the fried eggplant. Heat vinegar, stir in sugar and add to mixture. Blend in salt, pepper, oregano and simmer, covered, about 20 minutes. Stir frequently. Cool and serve at room temperature with other antipasto. Serves 6.

Volunteer
Washington County

BEEF CORNUCOPIAS
French

6 dried beef slices   3 tablespoons relish
6 tablespoons cream cheese

Make a mixture of cream cheese and relish. Spread on slices of dried beef. Roll in cornucopia fashion and chill before serving.

Volunteer
Putnam County

MADEIRA, EGGS AND MUSHROOMS
French

6 mushrooms, chopped   2 small onions, chopped
6 eggs, hard-boiled   Bread crumbs
1½ tablespoons Madeira   Salt and pepper to taste
1 teaspoon parsley, chopped   Toast rounds
1 tablespoon butter

Mix mushrooms, onions and parsley with yolks of hard-boiled eggs. Melt butter in pan. Add mushroom mixture, season with salt and pepper and Madeira. Cook until mushrooms and onions are tender. Then stuff eggs with mixture. Sprinkle with bread crumbs and add a dab of butter to each. Place on toast rounds and brown under broiler.

Volunteer
Genesee County

HUMOUS V'TECHINA
(Chick Pea and Sesame Paste Appetizer)
Israel

13¼-ounces chick peas (or 1
  large can cooked chick peas)
2 cloves garlic, crushed
  (you may use more)
Juice of 1 lemon (you may use
  2 lemons)

Salt to taste
Pepper or cayenne, to taste
1 pound sesame (techina) paste

Garnish:
3 tablespoons olive oil
3 tablespoons parsley, chopped
Paprika or cayenne

Vinegar pickles
Olives
Parsley sprigs

If using dry chick peas, soak them in water in a bowl or large jar, overnight, then cook them the next day for several hours until the skins come off. Save a few for garnish. Take the rest and puree it while hot. Stir in the remaining ingredients. (The consistency of chick peas should be like very heavy mayonnaise.) You may need to add a little hot water after adding the sesame paste, to dilute to desired thickness. If using canned chick peas instead of dry ones, the above mixture can be blended successfully in a blender. I have made it quickly in my blender but used less techina, about 8-10-ounces.

Note: This is a very nutritious dish, served in every restaurant and in private homes in Israel regularly, either as an appetizer, with "pita" bread or even as a main dish. It is served there in flat dishes with a swirl of olive oil and sprinkled with either parsley or paprika, sometimes with olives or pickles around the edges.

Volunteer
Tompkins County

Bread-Rolls

Scottish Immigrants

Ward E. Herrmann, Author of "SPANS OF TIME, Covered Bridges of Delaware County" has endeavored to collect and record what knowledge remains about covered bridge history. At one time there were more than 250 covered bridges in New York State and Delaware County was endowed with at least 57 different bridge sites.

Several tales found in his book center around the Scottish settlers, showing how they became known as "thrifty people". One private road toll gate was closely supervised by an old Scottish couple who argued with a customer about the charge of 2½¢ for a horse and buggy. The gatekeeper wanted 3¢ and the customer wanted 2¢. The gatekeeper said, "you just wait—I'll get your change". She hurried to the tool-shed, cut the penny in half and handed the customer his change, one half of a penny!

The covered bridges were a great place for children to play on rainy days and offered housewives a breezy place to dry their laundry.

Perhaps one of the funniest folklore tales of thrift involves a Scotsman, Robert Murray, who was a builder of several of these covered bridges. He lived in Bovina Center and worked in Delhi, a travellinig distance of approximately 10 miles. He walked barefoot to work each day, with his shoes tied over his shoulder so he wouldn't wear them out.

Interesting signs were found along the roads. On the top board of a wideboard fence there was an advertisement of sorts that read "Sallie buys her flour at Elwell's". The following day, on the second board was printed, "Everyone else buys theirs at Jones".

Our thanks to Ward E. Herrmann, author of "SPANS OF TIME, Covered Bridge of Delaware County, New York".

FRY BREAD
(Ghost Bread)
American Indian

6 cups flour
½ teaspoon salt

4 teaspoons baking powder
2½ cups milk

Mix flour, salt and baking powder together in a large bowl. Add milk and stir until all ingredients are mixed thoroughly. Make biscuit-size patties, ½-inch thick, with a hole in the center, using additional flour to keep from sticking. Fry in 2 or 3 tablespoons of shortening at medium heat. Turn over when brown and continue cooking until done. Additional shortening may be used until all the bread is cooked. Makes about 1½ dozen.

Note: Recipe can be used for fund raising at fairs or other activities. May be eaten with jam or jelly spread.

Tessie Snow
Cattaraugus County

PULLA
Scandinavian

2 cups milk
½ cup shortening
⅓ cup sugar
1½ teaspoons salt
2 yeast cakes
2 tablespoons water
   (to dissolve yeast)

2 eggs
10 cardamom seeds, crushed
   very fine
6 cups flour

Note: Cardamom seeds are put out by McCormick but not carried in all grocery stores, try Health Food Store.

Scald milk, add shortening, sugar and salt. When lukewarm, add yeast dissolved in lukewarm water. Add eggs, cardamom seeds and ½ of the flour. Beat it, add remaining flour. Let it rise in warm spot about 1 hour. Knead it, form 2 large loaves, or cut into strips for braiding. Let rise again for 45 minutes. Bake at 375 degrees for 20-30 minutes or until done, golden brown. Brush top with melted butter and sprinkle lightly with cinnamon/sugar mixture (optional).

Abby Hvitfelt
Delaware County

GREEK BREAD
Greek

1 package dry yeast	2 tablespoons sugar
⅓ cup warm water	1 teaspoon salt
1 cup milk	3¾-4 cups flour
¼ cup shortening	3 tablespoons butter, melted

Mix yeast and 105 degree-115 degree water until dissolved. In a saucepan, combine milk, shortening, sugar and salt. Heat. Stir until sugar and shortening are dissolved. Cool to lukewarm. Pour into bowl. Stir in 1 cup flour. Beat well. Add yeast. Beat until smooth. Gradually mix in remaining flour to make moderately stiff dough. Place on floured surface. Knead until smooth and satiny, about 10 minutes. Shape dough into ball. Place in lightly-oiled bowl. Turn to oil all sides. Cover. Put in warm place 1½ hours or until doubled. Punch dough down. Knead on floured surface 10 minutes. Place in oiled bowl. Cover. Let rise in warm place 1½ hours. Punch down. Place on floured surface. Divide in half. Shape each half into a ball. Let rest 10 minutes. Place dough on greased and floured baking sheet. Brush with melted butter. Let rise, uncovered, in warm place 1 hour or until doubled. Bake in 375 degree oven 45 minutes or until golden. Cool slightly before serving. Makes 2 loaves.

Volunteer
Cortland County

LIMPA RYE BREAD
Scandinavian

1 package dry yeast
¼ cup warm water
½ cup brown sugar, firmly packed
⅓ cup molasses
1 tablespoon Crisco shortening

1 tablespoon salt
1½ cups hot water
1 cup sifted all-purpose white flour
2 cups rye flour, sifted
3½ cups white flour, sifted

Dissolve 1 package dry yeast in ¼ cup warm water. Let stand 5 to 10 minutes, until lukewarm. Meanwhile, mix in large bowl the brown sugar, molasses, shortening and salt. Pour over this mixture 1½ cups hot water. Set aside until lukewarm, then blend in and beat until smooth 1 cup sifted white flour. Stir in yeast mixture and mix well. Measure 3 to 3½ cups sifted white flour. Add 2 cups rye flour to sugar mixture and beat until smooth. Beat in enough remaining flour to make a soft dough. Turn dough onto a very lightly floured board. Allow to rest 5 to 10 minutes. Knead gently. Form dough into ball and place in greased bowl, greasing top of dough. Let rise until doubled in bulk. Punch down with fist. Pull edges of dough in to center and turn dough over in bowl. Cover and let rise again until nearly doubled. Punch down and turn out on lightly floured surface. Grease baking sheet. Divide dough into two portions and shape into balls. Cover and rest 5 to 10 minutes. Remove to greased baking sheet. Cover and let rise until doubled. Bake at 375 degrees 25-30 minutes. Cool on racks. Grease tops of loaves with butter if soft crust is desired. Makes 2 large round loaves.

Mary Wescott Neidhardt
Madison County

ITALIAN SAUSAGE BREAD
Italian

1 pound bulk Italian hot
  sausage
1 1-pound package of Italian
  bread dough or pizza dough
1 pound Mozzarella cheese,
  shredded

1 egg, beaten
2 tablespoons spaghetti sauce
Melted butter
Garlic salt

Fry sausage in frying pan until well done and in small, crumbled pieces. Drain well.

Roll dough on a floured board or stretch with your hands to a 9-inch by 11-inch size.

Mix the sausage, shredded cheese, beaten egg and sauce in a bowl. Spread this mixture over the dough. Starting on the long side, roll the mixture in the dough to form a jelly-roll form. Pinch the ends and fold under. Place the bread on a greased cookie sheet. Be sure mixture is sealed into the dough or it may cook out in baking. Brush with melted butter. Sprinkle on garlic salt to taste. Bake at 350 degrees for 25 minutes or until golden.

Carol J. Salerno
Madison County

WELSH BREAD
(Bara Brith)
Welsh

6 cups white flour
½ teaspoon salt
2 teaspoons baking powder
1 teaspoon cinnamon
¼ teaspoon cloves or other
  desired spice
1 cup granulated sugar
1 cup brown sugar

1 cup shortening
11-ounces currants
11-ounces raisins
3 eggs
2 cups buttermilk
2 teaspoons baking soda
  dissolved in a little hot water

Mix dry ingredients, cutting in the fat. Add currants, raisins and mix well. Make a well in the center and add well beaten eggs, buttermilk and baking soda in water. Mix well. Makes 3 loaves in 9-inch x 5-inch x 3-inch baking tins or 5 loaves in 8-inch x 4-inch x 2-inch tins. Bake 1 hour at 300 degrees.

Mrs. Shirley Jones
Oneida County

BABKA
Polish Bread
Polish

9 cups flour (approximately),
  sifted
2 packages yeast
1 cup sugar
2 teaspoons salt
1 teaspoon cardamom
3 teaspoons lemon rind, grated

2 cups milk
½ cup warm water
1 cup shortening
6 eggs, beaten
1½ cups raisins

Mix together 3 cups flour, yeast, sugar, salt, cardamom and lemon rind. Heat milk, water and shortening. Add this to flour mixture. Beat for approximately 2 minutes with electric beaters. Gradually add eggs, raisins and rest of flour. Turn mixture out onto a floured board and knead until dough is smooth and elastic. Put dough into greased bowl and let rise until double. Take dough out, punch down and put into (4) loaf pans—greased and let rise again until double in bulk. Bake at 350 degrees for approximately 45 mintues.

Alice Van Heusen
Schenectady County

PASKA
"POLISH EASTER BREAD"
Polish

4 cups milk
2 packages dry yeast
1 cup sugar
5 egg yolks
1 tablespoon salt

½ cup butter, melted
10 cups flour
½ teaspoon vanilla
½ cup raisins (dark or light)
1 egg yolk

Scald milk in a large saucepan and let cool to lukewarm. Add dry yeast and 4 cups flour. Mix well. Let rise to a sponge mixture, about 2-4 hours. Add sugar, egg yolks, salt and the rest of the flour. Add the raisins and vanilla. Blend well and add melted butter. Work well into the dough and knead until dough leaves hands clean. Let rise until double in bulk. Shape and place in greased pans and let rise again. Brush top with 1 beaten egg yolk. Bake 1 hour at 350 degrees. Yield: 2 large or 4 regular size loaves.

Susie M. Polchowski
Washington County

IRISH BEER BREAD
Irish

3 cups self-rising flour
3 tablespoons sugar
1 12-ounce can of beer
   (inexpensive brand)

¼ cup raisins (optional—may
   use more or eliminate)
½ cup butter, melted

Preheat oven to 350 degrees. Grease well 2 loaf pans. In large bowl, sift flour and sugar together. While stirring well, add four ounces of beer, at a time. Mixture will be lumpy looking. Add raisins, if desired. Divide mixture into 2 well-greased loaf pans. Drizzle ½ cup melted butter over the tops. Bake in a 350 degree oven, for 50 minutes. Serve warm from the oven.

Mrs. Vincent Dollard
Sullivan County

IRISH SODA BREAD
Irish

3¼ cups flour
¼ cup sugar
1 teaspoon soda
1 teaspoon baking powder

¾ teaspoon salt
½ cup margarine
⅓ cup raisins
1⅓ cups buttermilk

Heat oven to 350 degrees. Combine dry ingredients. Cut in margarine until mixture resembles coarse crumbs. Add raisins and buttermilk, mixing just enough to moisten. Shape into ball. Knead on floured surface 10 times. Place on greased baking sheet. Shape into a round loaf, 2½-inches thick. Cut a ½-inch deep cross on top. Bake at 350 degrees for one hour. Serve warm.

Anne McDermott
Sullivan County

EASTER BREAD
Italian

2 packages dry yeast
¼ cup warm water
2 cups sugar
8 eggs

1 cup milk
½ cup liquid shortening
Flour
1 teaspoon flavoring

Dissolve yeast in warm water. Take sugar, eggs, milk, oil and beat together. Add yeast mixture. Flour rolling board, enough to make a well, and add mixture until you can knead the dough. Knead until smooth. Let rise about 3 hours or until double in size. Punch down and knead again. Shape into loaves. Cover and let rise again about 2 more hours. Brush with beaten egg yolk and bake about 20 minutes or until golden brown in 350 degree oven.

Mary Masters
Tompkins County

DANISH PUFF COFFEE CAKE
Scandinavian

Part I
½ cup butter
1 cup flour, sifted

2 tablespoons water

Part II
½ cup butter
1 cup water
1 teaspoon vanilla
1 cup flour

3 eggs
Powdered sugar frosting
Nuts (finely chopped)

Part I—Cut butter into flour. Sprinkle with water and mix with fork. Form into a ball and divide in half. Pat dough with hands into 2 long strips (12 x 3) about 3 inches apart on an ungreased cookie sheet.
Part II—Bring butter and water to boil in saucepan. Add vanilla and remove from heat. Stir in flour at once. When smooth and thick add eggs one at a time. Beat until smooth after each addition. Divide in half and spread evenly over each piece of pastry. Bake in 350 degree oven for 60 minutes until crisp and brown. Frost with powdered sugar frosting while warm. Sprinkle with nuts.

Mrs. Helen Penney
Tioga County

PANNU KAKKU
Finnish

1 tablespoon butter	Pinch of salt
3 eggs	¾ cup flour
3 cups milk	Anise seed
⅓ cup sugar	Wheat germ

Melt butter in a glass pan (approximately 13-inches x 8-inches) to be used in baking. Pour some of the melted butter into the batter mix.
Beat eggs slightly with a wisp beater. Add milk, sugar and salt. Add flour slowly and stir all ingredients together with wisp. Pour into the hot baking pan and sprinkle anise seed and wheat germ on top. Bake in 400 degree oven for 20 minutes. Reduce heat to 350 degrees for 10 additional minutes. Best served warm with coffee.

Lydia M. Hargrave
Tompkins County

INDIAN CORN PUDDING
American Indian

3 cups milk	½ teaspoon cinnamon
½ cup dark molasses	¼ teaspoon salt
⅓ cup yellow cornmeal	1 tablespoon butter
½ teaspoon ginger	

Preheat oven to 300 degrees. In heavy saucepan, mix milk and molasses together. Slowly add cornmeal, ginger, cinnamon and salt stirring constantly with a whisk to avoid lumps. Cook over low heat, stirring constantly until mixture is thick. (Approximately 10 minutes). Stir in butter and pour into a one-quart casserole. Bake uncovered for about one hour.

Note: This recipe can be adjusted to a sweeter fluffier pudding by adding one beaten egg and ¼ cup of sugar to above hot mixture, increasing butter one tablespoon and baking ½ hour longer. Serves 6.

Sue Mapledoram
Sullivan County

REAL DRESDEN STOLLEN
German

9 ounces almonds, blanched,
  peeled and finely chopped
22 ounces raisins
Peel of 6 lemons and 1 orange,
  grated
1 teaspoon vanilla
½ teaspoon cinnamon
¼ teaspoon ground cloves
¼ teaspoon nutmeg
½ cup rum

2 tablespoons dry yeast
1 cup candied grapefruit peel
4½ pounds flour
¾ quart milk
1 pound sugar
1¾ pounds butter (can be
  replaced at least half by
  margarine or shortening)
2 eggs

One hour before making the Stollen, grate the peel of the 6 lemons and 1 orange. Add the vanilla, cinnamon, cloves and nutmeg. Add the rum and place in tightly covered glass jar.

Dissolve the 2 tablespoons of dry yeast in warm milk or water until activated. Into the flour mix the milk, sugar, eggs and one half of the butter. (Keep the rest of the butter cold). Add the activated yeast. Knead well. Cover and let stand in warm place. After the dough has doubled in bulk, divide in 4 pieces. Incorporate the rest of the butter by chopping it in. Knead in the raisins, almonds, citrus peel and candied grapefruit peel. Roll into desired Stollen shape. Give a short time to rise. Bake in 350 degree oven for 1 hour. Watch for the last ½ hour to make sure it doesn't burn. When out of oven, brush with melted butter and dust with confectionary sugar.

Note: Put a pan of water in bottom of oven while baking.

Caroline Johnson
Warren County

DANISH PASTRIES
Scandinavian

1 cup milk
½ cup sugar
½ stick of margarine
1 heaping teaspoon salt

2 eggs
2 packages dry yeast (dissolved
   in ½ cup lukewarm water)
3-3½ cups flour

Filling:
1 cup crushed pineapple
½ cup sugar

1 tablespoon cornstarch

Scald milk, cool to lukewarm. Mix in sugar, margarine, salt, eggs, yeast (dissolved in ½ cup lukewarm water) and flour.
Let rise until doubled in bulk. Roll in oblong shape. Slice ¾ of a stick of *cold* margarine, thin, on ⅔ of the oblong rolled dough, fold dough. Roll and spread with margarine 3 times until margarine disappears. (This is what makes dough flaky). Cut in strips 1-inch thick and twist in pretzel shape. Let rise slowly in cool place. Bake 10-12 minutes in 400 degree oven.
After they are baked, fill. Mix crushed pineapple, sugar and cornstarch and cook until thick.

Note: Pastries can be frosted with a thin frosting and crushed nutmeats
       or left plain. Best when eaten warm.

Ruth Smithoover
Ontario County

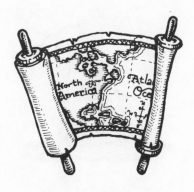

BAGELS
Polish

1½ cups, warm, *not hot,* water
(105-115 degrees)
1 package active dry yeast
3 tablespoons sugar

1 tablespoon salt
5 cups flour, sifted
Boiling water

Bagels are yeast rolls, shaped like a doughnut. After they are raised, they are simmered a half minute on each side in boiling water to give them a glaze when baked. Traditionally they are served toasted and spread with cream cheese and lox.

In warm large bowl, pour warm water and sprinkle yeast on top, add sugar and salt. Gradually beat in enough flour to make a soft dough. Turn out onto lightly floured board. Knead 10 minutes, until smooth and elastic and place in oiled bowl, turning dough to oil top. Place in cold oven with a saucepan of boiling water. Let rise for 15 minutes. Punch down dough. Roll dough out on a lightly floured board into a rectangle. Cut dough into 12 equal pieces with a floured knife. Flour hands, roll each piece between the palms into a rope 8 inches long. Dip ends into water, form a ring and pinch ends securely. Place 6 rings on waxed paper and the other 6 on another piece of waxed paper. Let rise 20 minutes or until puffy. Fill a shallow pan with water, bring to boil. Put the 6 rings of dough on the waxed paper into the boiling water, then remove paper. Cook a half minute on each side. With a slotted pancake turner remove to a paper towel. Place on baking sheets. Bake in moderately hot oven until brown. Remove to racks, split and serve. Yield: 12.

Eleanor Ardito
Delaware County

QUICK BISCUITS WITH CRACKLINGS
Hungarian

½ package yeast
2 tablespoons lukewarm water
1 teaspoon sugar
½ teaspoon salt
¼ teaspoon pepper
2 whole eggs

1 cup cracklings, coarsely
   chopped (can be thoroughly-
   rendered chicken, bacon, etc.)
½ cup sour cream
2½ cups flour, sifted
1 egg yolk

Preheat oven to 350 degrees. Soften yeast in lukewarm water, with sugar added, for 10 minutes. Blend in the salt, pepper, whole eggs, cracklings, and cream. Stir in flour and knead well. Roll out to ½-¾-inch thick. Using a 2-inch cookie cutter or top of a glass, cut into rounds and arrange on ungreased cookie sheet. Slash tops diagonally and brush with egg yolk and a few drops of water. Allow to rise 30 minutes. Bake at 350 degrees for 25 minutes or until brown. Yield: 24.

Betty Maythenyi
Sullivan County

PASSOVER ROLLS
Jewish

2 cups matzo meal
1 teaspoon salt
1 tablespoon sugar

1 cup water
½ cup peanut oil
4 eggs

Note: Matso meal may be found in large supermarkets.

Combine matzo meal with salt and sugar. Bring oil and water to a boil in saucepan over high heat. Add oil and water to matzo meal mixture and mix well with large spoon. Beat in the eggs thoroughly, one at a time. Allow this mixture to stand in bowl for 15 minutes.
With oiled hands, take a small amount of batter and shape into a roll (any desired shape, such as crescent, cylinder or muffin). Place each roll on a greased cookie sheet. This recipe usually makes 11 or 12 good-sized rolls, or 15 smaller ones. They can be made into bagel shapes. Bake the rolls at 375 degrees for 50 minutes until golden brown. This recipe can be made in about 1½ hours.
Note: Since bread and baked goods made with leavening such as yeast
      or baking powder are not permitted during the week of Passover
      observance these Passover rolls are a welcome addition to the
      holiday menus.

Volunteer
Tompkins County

Desserts

International Museum of Photography

GEORGE EASTMAN, FOUNDER

George Eastman, English descent, at the age of 14 had to leave school. With grim determination, he vowed to relieve the family's financial distress and to help out at home. He got a job as a messenger boy in an insurance firm at $3 per week and studied accounting at home evenings to get a better paying job. After five years in insurance work and at the age of 20, he was hired as a junior clerk at the Rochester Savings Bank.

George Eastman was always thrifty and saved. In the next seven years he had saved the sum of $3000 which he used for his start in the photograhic business.

The birth of the company was in the year 1881, when George Eastman leased the third floor of a building on State Street in Rochester and started to manufacture dry plates for sale. Difficulties were met and overcome. The thought ever present in Eastman's mind was to develop products that would simplify photography.

In order to do this he decided to make a new kind of camera. It was a box type camera, small and light, loaded with a roll of the stripping paper long enough for a hundred exposures. The price of the camera loaded and including a shoulder strap and case was $25. After exposure, the camera was sent to Rochester, where the exposed strip was removed, developed and printed, and a new one inserted at a charge of $10.

Anybody could "press the button," and Mr. Eastman's Company "would do the rest."

In 1891 the amateur transparent film was further improved by spooling it so it could be loaded into the camera by daylight. The camera did not have to be sent to Rochester to be re-loaded.

During Eastman's lifetime, he saw photography become a univeral language sending news across town, transmitting ideas between cultures, and recording personal experiences.

STRAWBERRIES ROMANOFF
French

10 fresh strawberries   ¼ cup whipped cream
2 ounces Port wine   ½ ounce Tia Maria
3 tablespoons powdered sugar

Let strawberries stand in port wine for a few hours. Add the sugar, whipped cream and Tia Maria, mix well until creamy. Serve in a very cold Champagne glass or over ice cream.

Note: Serve Champagne to accompany this dessert.

Joy Quimby
Onondaga County

GULE
(Covered Plums)
Slavic

4 boiled potatoes   Pinch of salt
2 egg yolks   1 large can pitted plums
2½ cups flour

Combine mashed potatoes, eggs, flour and salt. (Save a little for working the dough). Knead dough so that it is workable and not sticky, adding flour as needed. Roll on floured board and cut into squares big enough to work dough around plums to cover completely. Put gule in boiling water and cook about 5-8 minutes. Drain and cover with fried bread crumbs or sweetened ground poppy seeds.

Volunteer
Fulton County

ROMFROMAGE
(Rum Dessert)
Scandinavian

6 egg yolks
1 cup sugar
1 tablespoon gelatin
1 tablespoon cold water

½ cup boiling water
½ cup rum
4 egg whites
½ pint whipping cream

Beat egg yolks until thick and lemon colored, gradually beat in 1 cup sugar. Soak gelatin in 1 tablespoon cold water. Add boiling water and stir until dissolved. Add egg yolk mixture and blend well. Add rum. Mix again. Beat egg whites stiff. Whip cream. Add egg whites and whipped cream to egg yolk mixture. Put in a bowl. Chill for 2-4 hours. Serve with whipped cream. Serves 6.

Mrs. Louise Christensen
Yates County

PAVLOVA
Australia

Pinch of salt
4 egg whites
¼ teaspoon cream of tartar

1 cup sugar
3 drops vanilla essence
Fruit salad or strawberries

Add salt to egg whites. (These should be at room temperature), whip until stiff. Add cream of tartar and whip until whites hold a point, gradually adding sugar whipping well. Add 3 drops of vanilla essence. Place mixture in lightly greased pie plate—building up the sides. Bake for 1 hour in 275 degree oven. Allow to cool. When ready to eat fill meringue shell with fruit salad and fresh whipped cream.

Coralie North
Franklin County

BAKED APPLES AND MINCEMEAT
Australia

6 large apples
2 tablespoons lemon juice
2 tablespoons water

Brown sugar
Butter
Mincemeat

Remove core, peel top of apples. Stand in shallow dish. Pour lemon juice and water around and fill centers with mincemeat. Top with sugar and a little butter. Bake in 350 degree oven, baste once or twice until tender, approximately 40 minutes.

Lorna Collins
Franklin County

PLUM PUDDING
English

1 pound flour
1 pound suet, chopped fine
½ pound bread crumbs
½ teaspoon of cinnamon,
   cloves, allspice, nutmeg and
   mace
1 teaspoon salt

2 cups sugar
½ pound citron
1½ pounds large raisins
1½ pounds currants
6 eggs
1½ cups milk

Mix flour, suet, salt, crumbs, spices, and sugar together. Add fruit. Beat eggs and milk. Mix well with dry ingredients. Scald pudding cloth, dust with flour. Place pudding in cloth. Tie tightly and put in boiling water and boil constantly for 6 hours. Be sure water covers pudding while boiling. When adding more water, be certain it is boiling.
Boil 4 hours more on the day served, 10 hours boiling is necessary for good results. Serve with the hard or liquid sauce or whipped cream. Place plate in bottom of saucepan while boiling to prevent sticking.

Volunteer
Lewis County

FLAN
Spanish

5 eggs   1 teaspoon vanilla
1 cup milk   ½ cup sugar
1 can condensed milk

Beat until frothy the 5 eggs, 1 cup milk, 1 can of condensed milk, and 1 teaspoon vanilla. Meanwhile liquify the ½ cup of sugar in a sauce pan over a low heat, and when ready pour into a small bread pan coating all five sides with the liquid sugar. Before the sugar coating has a chance to harden, pour the egg mixture in the pan, and set the pan into a larger second pan which has been filled with one inch of water. Bake both pans in a 350 degree oven for one hour, or until an inserted knife blade comes out clean. Invert the pan immediately upon removing it from the oven and serve hot or chilled. Serves 8-10.

Volunteer
Orleans County

RED FRUIT PUDDING
(SAFT KRAM)
Scandinavian

12 ounces red currants   2-3 level tablespoons corn flour
12 ounces black currants or   (cornstarch)
  raspberries   Cold water
1½ pints water (3¾ cups)   1½ ounces almonds, blanched
12 ounces sugar   and slivered
                                Cream

Wash the fruit and place it in a sauce pan with water. Simmer until tender and rub through a sieve. Pour juice back into the sauce pan and bring to a boil. Add the sugar and the corn flour, stirred to a thin paste with a little cold water. Boil for 2-3 minutes. When cool pour into a glass serving dish, sprinkle a little sugar on top to prevent skin from forming, sprinkle almonds over the top and leave to cool down completely. Serve with sweetened thick or thin cream in a separate dish.

Note: This is also good served over French vanilla ice cream.

Mrs. Frank Kozel
Columbia County

BIRD-MILK
Hungarian

5 eggs
5 tablespoons sugar
1 quart milk
1 tablespoon rum
  (or rum extract)

3 tablespoons blanched
  almonds, chopped

Separate egg-white from yolk, put them in 2 mixing bowls. Whip egg-whites until peaks form. Mix yolk with sugar until smooth and foamy. Heat milk in pot to boiling. With soup-spoon take out a spoonful from whipped egg-white and put in slowly to boiling milk. Repeat until all egg-whites are in milk. Turn each once (takes about 2 minutes each). Put them out on a platter. Take milk off from heat, and slowly, constantly stirring, pour in the whipped yolks. Put mixture back on heat and stir constantly until mixture starts to boil. Take off heat right away. Add rum. Set pot in cold water and stir until cool. Pour in serving bowl, arrange egg-whites on top. Sprinkle with blanched chopped almonds. Keep covered in refrigerator until needed. Serves 5.

Mrs. Andrew N. Juhasz
Schuyler County

CHOCOLATE FONDUE
Swiss

4 ounces butter
6 ounces unsweetened
  chocolate
11 ounces granulated sugar

1 cup half and half
⅛ teaspoon salt
¼ cup Creme De Cacao

In a sauce pan melt the butter and chocolate over a low heat. Add the sugar, half and half, and salt to the mixture. Cook over a medium heat for five minutes or until thickened, stirring constantly. (At this point, the mixture may be covered and refrigerated until needed, when it should be re-warmed). Just before serving, stir in the Creme De Cacao.
Serve in a fondue pot accompanied by pound cake squares and bite-size pieces of fresh fruit (apples, melons, peaches, pineapples, strawberries). Serves 8.

Frank Cutson
Orleans County

NOODLE KUGEL
(Pudding)
Jewish

1 8-ounce package broad
  noodles
4 eggs
2 tablespoons all-purpose flour
1 teaspoon salt
1 teaspoon baking powder
1 cup sugar
2 ounces butter (½ bar)
1 cup yellow raisins

1 small can crushed pineapple
  with juice
2 apples, peeled, cored and
  sliced medium thin
½ orange-juice, grate skin
1 teaspoon almond flavoring
Brown sugar and cinnamon mix
  for topping

Preheat oven to 350 degrees. Cook noodles according to package directions; drain. In separate bowl, beat eggs well; add cooked noodles. In another bowl, mix flour, salt, baking powder and sugar together. Melt butter; add to noodle-egg mixture; add flour mixture, raisins, pineapple with juice, apples, orange juice and grated skin, almond extract. Grease 3 quart baking dish. Place all ingredients in baking dish and sprinkle with sugar-cinnamon mix. Bake one hour. When casserole begins to brown, cover with foil for remaining time. Upon removal from oven—remove foil to let steam escape to prevent a watery product.

Note: Peel and slice apples last to avoid discoloration.

Ilene B. Haym
Ontario County

DATE PUDDING
English

4 eggs
1 cup sugar
1 cup dates, chopped
1 cup nuts, chopped

2 tablespoons lemon juice
½ cup flour
½ teaspoon baking powder

Separate eggs. Beat whites with ½ cup sugar until very stiff. Set aside. Beat yolks, add ½ cup sugar. Add dates, nuts, lemon juice to beaten yolks. Stir in flour and baking powder. Fold in whites. Bake in greased 1½-quart casserole set in hot water for 1 hour at 325 degrees. May be made day before serving. Garnish with whipped cream. Serves 10-12.

Marian Clawson
Oswego County

STEAMED BLACK PUDDING WITH SAUCE
German

1 egg
1 cup dark molasses
1 teaspoon ginger
1 teaspoon soda

⅔ cup boiling water
1½ cups flour, sifted
2 tablespoons melted fat

Sauce:
2 eggs
½ cup butter, melted

2 cups confectioners' sugar
1 teaspoon vanilla

In large bowl, beat eggs, add molasses. Mix soda in water. Add to egg mixture. Add sifted flour, salt, ginger, beat in melted fat. Pour in greased pan. Cover tight. Steam 1¼ hours. Serve hot.

Sauce: Beat together all ingredients until thick and creamy. Serve warm.

Mrs. Frederick Haas
Madison County

CRANBERRY NOODLE PUDDING
German

1 pound broad noodles
½ pound butter
3 eggs, beaten
1 pint sour cream
1 pound cottage cheese

1 cup sugar
1 teaspoon salt
½ teaspoon cinnamon
Corn flake crumbs
1 can whole cranberry sauce

Boil noodles for 8 minutes and drain. Melt butter in 2-quart baking dish. Beat eggs until fluffy. Mix all ingredients thoroughly with noodles in large bowl. Then put half of mixture into the pan with melted butter. Spread can of whole cranberry sauce over noodles. Put remaining half of noodles and cheese mixture over this. Sprinkle with corn flake crumbs. Bake in 350 degree oven until golden brown, about one hour.

Syd Hinderstein
Greene County

BUDAPEST CHOCOLATE
Hungarian

½ pound semisweet chocolate
1¼ cups sugar
1 tablespoon vanilla
2 tablespoons rum

1½ cups cream (heavy)
5 egg yolks
5 egg whites

With electric mixer, mix in rotation the semisweet chocolate (which has been melted in a double boiler over hot water), sugar, vanilla, rum and ½ cup of the cream (unwhipped). Slightly beat the egg yolks and mix. Beat the egg whites very stiff and fold in. Whip the remaining cup of heavy cream and fold in. Pour into sherbet glasses, chocolate pot dé cream cups or a large soufflé dish. Serve topped with whipped cream and either finely chopped nuts or curls of chocolate. Serves 8-12, depending on size of serving dish used.

Pat Gerber
Erie County

ENGLISH TRIFLE
English

Lady fingers
2 tablespoons rum or sherry
jam or jelly (enough to spread on lady fingers)
2 packages gelatin (different flavors)

1 package vanilla pudding
Whipped cream
Candied cherries
Blanched almonds

Spread jam between lady fingers and place in bottom of glass bowl. Spoon sherry or rum over lady fingers. Make pudding and both gelatins. Spoon one gelatin over lady fingers. Chill and also chill pudding.
Before serving, spoon vanilla pudding over gelatin and lady fingers. Cut up second gelatin and spoon over vanilla pudding. Garnish with whipped cream, cherries and almonds.

Alice Hotchkiss
Albany County

LAND OF CHRIST CHRISTMAS PUDDING
Palestinian

1 cup flour
1 teaspoon baking powder
½ teaspoon soda
½ teaspoon salt
1 teaspoon cinnamon
¼ teaspoon allspice
¼ teaspoon cloves
½ cup nuts, chopped

½ cup raisins
½ cup fruit cocktail, drained
1 cup milk
1 cup dry bread crumbs
½ cup margarine, melted
½ cup molasses
½ cup brown sugar

Hard Sauce:
⅓ cup butter
1 cup confectioners' sugar

½ teaspoon lemon extract
⅔ teaspoon vanilla

In large bowl mix flour, baking powder, soda, salt, cinnamon, allspice and cloves. Add nuts, raisins and fruit. Heat milk and pour over bread crumbs. Pour the melted margarine, molasses and brown sugar into the milk and breadcrumb mixture. Add to dry ingredients and stir until smooth. Pour into well-greased mold or pan (or use 1 to 1½ pound cans or other small boilable containers) filling two thirds full. Tie several thicknesses of wax paper over the top. Place on rack in deep kettle filled with boiling water to one half the depth of the mold. Cover kettle and steam 2½ hours, adding water as needed. Serve hot.

To Flame:
Pour a few drops of lemon extract on a lump of sugar and place on top of pudding. Arrange sprigs of holly around it, and just before serving light the moistened sugar.

Hard Sauce:
Cream butter and sugar till very light. Add flavoring and chill. Serve a spoonful with each portion.

Note: The traditional Christmas pudding contains spices and fruits because long ago the Three Wise Men brought them from the East as gifts to the Christ Child. The flame on the pudding is a token that the "light of the world" was made visible to human eyes on that first Christmas day.

Mrs. Lucille White Cutting
Clinton County

POLISH PINEAPPLE PASTRY
Polish

Crumbs:

½ cup sugar   ¼ pound butter or margarine

Dough:

3 cups flour   1 teaspoon vanilla
1 cup butter or margarine   ¼ teaspoon salt
3 egg yolks, blended   2 packages dry yeast
1 cup milk, cooked

1 21-ounce can Pineapple Pie filling (or any of their other selections you prefer)

Glaze:

1 egg yolk   Splash of vanilla

Make crumbs and chill. Mix ingredients of dough and knead until well mixed. Grease cookie sheet. Cut dough in half and roll out with rolling pin. Place in cookie sheet. Spread the pie filling evenly over dough. Roll out other half of dough and place over pie filling as you would with regular pie. Raise for 45 minutes. Glaze surface. Separate crumb mixture into large crumb-type consistency and sprinkle over top. Bake in 350 degree oven for 15 minutes, then continue baking until golden brown. Cool and serve.

Emilia Czyryca
Wyoming County

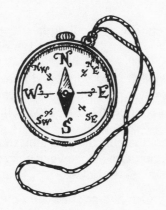

APFELSHNITTEN
(Apple Strips)
Austria

2½ cups flour
1 teaspoon salt
1 tablespoon sugar
1 cup Crisco
1 egg, separated
⅔ cup milk

⅔ cup cereal flakes, crushed
    (corn flakes, wheaties, etc.)
5 cups apples, peeled and
    sliced
1 cup sugar
1 teaspoon cinnamon

Preheat oven to 400 degrees. In large bowl mix flour, salt and one table-spoon sugar. Cut in Crisco. Mix together egg yolk and milk and add to crumble mixture. Form into ball. Take out half and roll out on floured board. Put this on 15 x 10-inch pan. Place cereal mixture into bottom, distribute apples and add sugar and spices. Roll out rest of dough and cover, as in a pie. Brush top with beaten egg white. Bake 40 minutes. Yield: 25-2 x 3-inch pieces.

Note: Family favorite. Great for the lunchpail.

Mrs. Audrey J. Peach
Onondaga County

BLINTZES
Jewish

Crepe:
½ cup flour
1 cup water

3 eggs
Enough butter to grease pan

Filling:
2 packages farmer's cheese
    (1 pound each)

2 eggs
Salt to taste

Mix flour and water together, add eggs, and beat well. Melt butter and grease 5-inch frying pan over medium heat. Use one cooking spoon (1½-2 tablespoons) of mixture for each crepe—do not turn. Flip out onto clean cloth. (A linen dish towel works well).

Mix filling ingredients together and use one tablespoon of filling per crepe. After all are filled and wrapped like an envelope, fry in butter on both sides until golden brown. Yield: 15-16 blintzes.

Note: Serve with sour cream and-or strawberry preserves.

Mrs. Joseph Rose
Columbia County

CHOUX AUX FRAISES
(Cream puffs with strawberries)
French

Pastry Base:

1 cup water
4 tablespoons butter, cut into
    small pieces
¼ teaspoon salt

1 tablespoon sugar
1 cup all-purpose flour, sifted
4 eggs

Filling:

1 cup sugar
5 egg yolks
¾ cup flour
1 cup milk, simmering

1 cup heavy cream, simmering
1 teaspoon vanilla extract
1 quart strawberries (fresh)
½ cup red currant jelly, melted

Place water, butter, salt and sugar in a heavy saucepan. Adjust heat so that the butter has completely melted when the water boils. Remove pan from heat as soon as the water boils. Add the flour all at once and stir vigorously. Return the pan to a moderate heat for two minutes until the dough can be formed into a ball. Remove the pan from the heat and add eggs *one at a time.* Beat each egg well into the mixture before adding the next egg. Butter and flour two cookie sheets. Using 2 spoons, form balls of dough about the size of an egg and place 3 inches apart. Bake in a 375 degree oven for 25 minutes until puffed and golden. In the meantime, prepare the filling: Beat the sugar and egg yolks until thick and lemon colored. Beat in the flour. Stir in simmering milk and cream. Place in a saucepan over moderate heat and stir continuously to form a medium thick custard. Cool the custard. It will become thicker as it cools. Slice the top from each cream puff. Fill with cooled custard and top with strawberries. Brush strawberries with melted red currant jelly to make them shine. Decorate plates with remaining strawberries glazed with jelly. Serves 8.

Kathleen Duley
Clinton County

STRUDEL
Jewish

Strudel Dough #I (Stretched Sheet):

2 cups flour
¼ teaspoon salt
White of one egg

⅔ cup warm water
   (approximately)
⅓ cup shortening, melted

Sift the flour and the salt, add the egg white, mix a little, and then add sufficient water to make a soft dough. Knead well on a board until no longer sticky, tossing and stretching the dough to make it elastic. Brush with shortening and cover with a warm bowl for about an hour. When ready, place on a well-floured tablecloth on a large table and roll a little. Brush again with some of the melted shortening, and with the hands under the dough, palms down, pull and stretch the dough gently from the center. Then using the fingertips, palms up, pull gradually around the edges until the sheet is as thin as tissue paper and as large as the table. The rest of the shortening should be used to sprinkle over the sheet after the filling has been spread, and to brush the top of the rolled strudel before baking. Bake in a well greased pan.

Strudel Dough #II (Rolled Sheet):

2 cups flour
½ teaspoon baking powder
¼ teaspoon salt

1 egg
¼ cup shortening, melted
6 tablespoons warm water

Beat the egg, add the oil and the water and then the flour mixed with the salt and the baking powder. Knead lightly until the dough is very soft, a little oily, but no longer sticky. Cover and set in a warm place for at least one hour. Place on a floured tablecloth and roll out as thin as possible. Finish by stretching and pulling gently with the fingertips until the sheet is as thin as tissue paper. A smaller piece of dough can be rolled thin more successfully than a larger piece, so break the dough in half and roll and fill each part separately.

Dry Fruit Strudel:

¾ pound dried apricots
¾ cup sugar
1 lemon, grated
1 orange, grated
1 cup walnuts, crushed
¾ cup sugar

½ teaspoon cinnamon
1 cup white raisins
1 cup cake or bread crumbs,
   fine
1 tablespoon shortening, melted
1 cup coconut

Use strudel dough I or II as preferred, adding one teaspoon sugar to the dough. The ingredients of the first column make a delicious filling. However, any fruit preserve may be substituted. After washing well, cover the dried

Strudel (continued)

fruit with boiling water and soak overnight. Drain off the water and chop fine. Grate a whole lemon and a whole orange, rind and meat, and add half to the chopped fruit together with the sugar. Mix until thoroughly blended. Combine the other half of the grated lemon and orange with all the remaining ingredients.

After the dough has been stretched as thin as possible, spread the nut mixture evenly over the entire sheet. Drip a little melted shortening over all. Spread the fruit mixture in a thin line across one end of the sheet about four inches from the edge. Fold this edge over the fruit, raise the tablecloth and roll. Place the rolls in well greased pans and let them stand about a quarter of an hour. With a sharp knife slice the strudel into one inch pieces, but do not cut all the way through. Bake in a hot oven (400 degrees) for about an hour.

Bess Grocoff and Sis Kaplan
Monroe County

FASTNACHT KUGELN
(Traditional Donuts for Ash Wednesday)
German

1 cake yeast
1 cup lukewarm milk (105-115
  degrees)
6 cups flour

2 teaspoons salt
2 tablespoons sugar
¾ cup soft butter
6 eggs

Dissolve yeast cake in milk. Sift flour, salt and sugar into a large bowl. Make a hole in the center. Add butter and eggs into hole. Mix together. Add more flour if too sticky. Punch down. Let rise 35 minutes. Punch down. Let rest 10 minutes. Roll dough out ¼-inch thick. Cut out 2-inch circles. Let rise 20-30 minutes. Fry both sides in deep fat (370 degrees). Drain on paper toweling placed on brown paper. While warm roll in granulated sugar.

Note: This recipe came from Germany and has been translated into English so the family could keep the tradition for Ash Wednesday.

Mrs. Brian Cook
Monroe County

PARTY NUT ROLLS
Polish

3 cups flour	1 cup sugar
3 teaspoons baking powder	3 eggs
¼ teaspoon salt	1½ teaspoons vanilla
1 stick soft margarine	4 tablespoons Pet milk

Sift flour, salt and baking powder 3 times. Put into a large bowl and add the sugar. Using hands mix well but gently. Add the soft margarine, and mix well—like mixing for a pie crust. Add the eggs, one at a time mixing gently and stir in the vanilla. Add the milk and mix well with hands. Let dough stand for 1 hour. Take small amount (heaping tablespoon) and roll out on a floured board. Cut into squares (3-inch x 3-inch). Spread with nut filling and roll as you would for a jelly roll. Grease cookie sheet lightly and place bottom side down each roll. Bake at 350 degrees for 6-8 minutes. While rolls are still warm, sprinkle white sugar over the rolls. May be served plain or may be frosted.

Nut Filling:

1½ cups nuts, ground fine	5 tablespoons powdered sugar
1 egg	¾ cup warm milk (always use
3 tablespoons honey	warm milk to spread filling
	easily).

Mix all ingredients together—use teaspoon or slightly more of filling for each roll.

Bernice Padlo
Cattaraugus County

BOHEMIAN PASTRY
Bohemia

1 envelope dry yeast
1 teaspoon sugar
¼ cup warm water
2 cups flour
½ teaspoon salt

¾ cup butter
2 eggs
½ cup sugar
1 teaspoon vanilla
1 cup nuts, crushed

Sprinkle yeast and the 1 teaspoon sugar over warm water. Let stand until yeast is softened. Sift together flour and salt. Cut in butter until mixture has texture of corn meal. Separate eggs. Mix yolks with yeast and add to flour mixture. Form into ball. Beat egg whites until slightly stiffened. Slowly beat in sugar. Continue beating until very stiff. Fold in vanilla. Divide dough in half. Roll out each half on floured surface into a 9 x 12-inch rectangle. Spread each rectangle with half of egg white mixture, sprinkle with nuts. Roll up, starting from long side. Transfer to greased baking sheet. Make a ½-inch deep cut down the center of each roll. Bake immediately at 375 degrees for about 20 minutes or until lightly browned. Sprinkle with powdered sugar.

Note: These keep about two days in the cupboard, or in the freezer for one month.

Margot Morgan
Wyoming County

CHOCOLATE COVERED MINT "PADDIES"
Irish

1 pound confectioners' sugar
¼ cup butter, melted
2½ tablespoons warm water
15 drops oil of peppermint

4 squares unsweetened
  chocolate
½ brick paraffin wax

Note: You may purchase Oil of peppermint at your Drug store.
Place confectioners' sugar in large mixing bowl, melt butter, remove from heat and add water and oil of peppermint. Pour onto sugar. Mix with hands until soft. Form patties (paddies) with hands. Make 1½-2-inches flat. Cool in refrigerator. Place 4 squares chocolate and ½ brick paraffin into double boiler, melt over medium heat. When chocolate is smooth, dip paddies, place onto wax paper at room temperature.

Mrs. Tony Montanaro
Oswego County

HUMANTOSHAN—FOR HOLIDAY OF PURIM
Jewish

Cookie:

3 teaspoons baking powder
3 eggs
1 cup sugar
1 teaspoon salt
1 cup shortening

1 teaspoon almond extract
Juice and rind from 1 lemon
Juice and rind from 1 orange
3 cups flour

Note: Prune Filling is called Lekvar in Kosher Food Section.

Prune Filling:

1 1-ounce jar prune filling
1 orange, grated rind and juice
1 lemon, grated rind and juice

1 cup walnuts, chopped
¼ cup bread crumbs

In a large bowl, mix baking powder, eggs, sugar, salt, shortening, almond extract, grated orange rind and orange juice, grated lemon rind and lemon juice. Add flour a handful at a time (approximately ½ cup), kneading as you add. Continue adding flour and kneading until dough feels cool and rollable. Roll dough, cut with a large round cookie cutter. Set aside.
For filling, mix prune filling, orange rind and orange juice, lemon rind and lemon juice, walnuts and bread crumbs.
Place 1 tablespoon of prune filling in center of dough, fold over and pinch together to form a triangle covering filling with cookie dough. Bake at 375 degrees for 20 minutes or until golden in color.

Eileen Aronson
Saratoga County

SPRITZ COOKIES
Norway

1 cup soft butter or margarine
⅔ cup sugar
3 egg yolks
1 teaspoon vanilla

2½ cups flour, sifted
¼ teaspoon salt
Red and green candied cherries

Can be frozen. Mix first 4 ingredients well, blend in flour and salt. Force through spritz gun or cookie press onto cookie sheets. Decorate with bits of cherries. Bake in hot oven 400 degrees, 7-10 minutes. Yield: 6 dozen.

Betty Shenkle
Albany County

CUCIDATE
(Christmas Sugar Cookies)
Italian

Cookie Dough:

1½ cups shortening
1½ cups sugar
5 eggs
4½ cups flour
2 tablespoons baking powder

½ teaspoon salt
½ cup milk
Few drops anise flavor
1 teaspoon vanilla

Filling:

2 pounds figs
1 pound raisins
1 pound dates
1 package toasted almonds
1 can walnut meats
1 can crushed pineapple

1 cup sugar
1 tablespoon cinnamon
½ teaspoon cloves
1 teaspoon anise flavor
1 large package chocolate chips
1 orange rind, grated

Cream shortening and sugar, add eggs one at a time. Sift flour, baking powder and salt three times, then add to mixture, alternately with milk, anise flavor and vanilla. Refrigerate overnight. Roll out to ⅛-inch thick, cut into 3-inch wide strips, fill and fold so ends stick together. Bake at 375 degrees about 25 minutes.

Filling:
Grind first 5 ingredients in food chopper. Add last seven ingredients and mix well.

Sadie Nau
Monroe County

LEMON ITALIAN COOKIES
Italian

2 cups flour, sifted once
3 teaspoons baking powder
4 tablespoons sugar
4 heaping tablespoons
  shortening

½ cup milk
1 egg
1 teaspoon lemon extract

Sift flour; add baking powder and sugar; sift again. Cut in shortening, add milk, egg and lemon extract. Blend thoroughly. Flour hands; pinch out about 1 teaspoon dough and roll into ball, repeat process and place on greased cookie sheets 2½ inches apart. Bake 375 degrees 10-15 minutes.

Frosting: Mix together 2 cups confectioners' sugar, ⅓ cup shortening and enough heated milk to make a spreading consistency. Put on cookies and diversify your sprinkling decoration—nutmeats, coconut, colored candies, etc.

Volunteer
Rockland County

DANISH CHRISTMAS COOKIES
Danish

2 cups shortening
2 cups sugar
2 teaspoons vanilla
2 eggs, well beaten

4 cups sifted flour
1 teaspoon soda
½ teaspoon salt
1 teaspoon cream of tartar

Combine shortening, sugar and vanilla. Add beaten eggs and continue to blend. Sift flour, soda, salt and cream of tartar. Add gradually to first mixture. Chill dough for a few minutes. Roll out thinly. Cut into desired shapes. Place 2 inches apart on cookie sheet. Bake 375 degrees 8-10 minutes. Yield: 6½ dozen.

Volunteer
Lewis County

GRYBAI
(Mushroom Cookies)
Lithuanian

1 cup honey
½ cup sugar
¼ cup butter
4 tablespoons brown sugar
2 eggs
¼ cup sour cream
1½ teaspoons baking soda
5½ cups flour, sifted

½ teaspoon lemon rind
½ teaspoon orange rind
½ teaspoon cinnamon
¼ teaspoon ginger
¼ teaspoon ground cloves
⅛ teaspoon nutmeg
⅛ teaspoon cardamom

Preheat oven to 350 degrees. Heat honey, until just warm. In medium sized bowl add sugar, butter, brown sugar, eggs and sour cream, stir well. Add honey and baking soda, stir well. Add slowly flour, grated rinds and spices. Dough will thicken. Knead in remaining flour. Divide dough in half, cover other half with wax paper. Form pieces of dough into various sized mushroom caps, making small indentations in flat side with finger tip. Place on cookie sheet. Form stems by rolling pieces of dough to size of pencil or small finger—1½ inches in length. Make enough stems to correspond to amount of caps. Bake at 350 degrees for 10 minutes or until lightly browned. Cool. Dip end of stem in icing, fit into indentation in cap. Dip other end in icing and then into some poppy seeds.

Mushrooms may be iced with 2 cups sugar, ⅓ cup water, boiled until thick and bubbly. Cool, add ½ teaspoon vinegar and beat. 1 square baking chocolate may be added to half the icing to make brown coated mushrooms as well as white coated mushrooms.

Mrs. Anna Love
Montgomery County

SPRINGERLES
German

Note: For this recipe you need springerle rolling pin or board

4 eggs
4 cups confectioners' sugar, sifted

2 teaspoons anise extract
4 cups flour, sifted
1 teaspoon soda

Beat eggs until light. Add sugar gradually and beat at high speed for 15 minutes or until mixture is like soft meringue. Add anise extract. Put in large bowl and gradually add flour and soda sifted together. Work in by hand, add more flour if necessary. Cover bowl tightly—let stand 15 minutes. Divide dough into thirds and roll each piece ⅓ of 1-inch thick. Let stand 1 minute. Dust rolling pin with flour; roll over cookies. Cut cookies apart. Place on lightly floured surface. Let stand overnight. Grease cookie sheets well, brush excess flour from cookies. Bake at 300 degrees for about 20 minutes or until lightly browned. Store in airtight container or freeze. Yield: 6 dozen.

Volunteer
Hamilton County

KOURABIEDES
(Greek Cookies)
Greek

2 cups sweet butter
¾ cup confectioners' sugar
1 egg yolk
1 jigger Brandy or Cognac

4½ cups flour, sifted
Whole cloves
Confectioners' sugar
   (for topping)

Cream butter and sugar until very light. Gradually beat in egg yolk and brandy. Blend in flour to make a soft dough. With floured hands shape dough into 1½-inch balls and stud each ball with 1 whole clove. Place on baking sheets and bake in a 350 degree oven for 15 minutes. Cool slightly and sift confectioners' sugar over cookies. Yield: 4-6 dozen.

Note: *REMOVE* WHOLE CLOVE BEFORE EATING.

Mrs. James Winterbottom
St. Lawrence County

GERMAN BLACK AND WHITE COOKIES
German

¼ pound of butter	1 package of Oetker Vanilla
½ cup of sugar	Flavored Pudding & Pie
2 eggs	Filling mix (1½ ounces)*
Dash of salt	3-4 tablespoons milk
1 teaspoon vanilla or Oetker's	2 teaspoons baking powder
vanillan sugar (pkg)*	2 cups flour

*Note: Oetker's Pudding and vanilla sugar can be found in Gourmet Shops
or German Meat Market or delicatessan

Icing:

⅓ package of confectioners'	2-3 tablespons of hot water
sugar	

(Mix together to a spreading consistency.)

Cream butter and add sugar, eggs, salt, vanilla flavor and mix well together in large bowl. Put pudding mix into a cup, add milk and mix together. Add this to the batter in large bowl. Mix baking powder into flour and add slowly to batter and mix so that batter is thick enough to spoon. Drop by spoonfuls onto greased (butter) baking sheet. Bake at 350 degrees approximately 10-15 minutes until lightly browned. Turn upside down and while still warm, spread white icing first on half of the cookie and then add cocoa to icing mix and spread other half of cookie with chocolate icing.

Marie Delardi
Rockland County

OLD FASHIONED SWEDISH BUTTER COOKIES
Scandinavian

1 cup butter (not margarine)	2½ cups flour
1 egg	1 teaspoon baking soda
1½ cups confectioners' sugar	1 teaspoon cream of tartar

Cream butter, egg, and sugar until fluffy. Mix and add remaining ingredients. Chill for 1 hour in refrigerator. Roll out thin and cut with fancy cookie cutters. Place on greased sheet and bake at 350 degrees for 10 minutes.

Alice Peterson
Chautauqua County

GIOVANNINA'S CHOCOLATE COOKIES
Italian

7 cups flour
1½ cups granulated sugar
¾ cup shortening
7 teaspoons baking powder
2 teaspoons cinnamon
1 teaspoon salt
1 teaspoon ground cloves
⅔ cup cocoa

½ cup cocomalt powder or
   malted milk powder
Rind of 1 orange
6 eggs
1 cup walnuts, coarsely
   chopped
1 cup milk

In large mixing bowl, mix first three ingredients until well blended. Add baking powder, cinnamon, salt, ground cloves, cocoa, malted milk powder, orange rind, and 6 eggs. Mix well. Then add 1 cup of coarsely chopped walnuts and enough milk to make stiff dough. (About 1 cup.) Heat oven to 325 degrees. Roll mix into balls about 1-inch. Place on ungreased cookie sheet, approximately 1-inch apart. Bake 20-25 minutes.
To Frost: Use well sifted confectioners' sugar, add a few drops of milk, flavor with vanilla extract.

Note: A good cookie to send away in packages.

Mary J. Bonady
Steuben County

JAN HAGEL KOEKJES
(Johnny Buckshot Cookies)
Dutch

1 cup butter
1 cup sugar
1 egg yolk
1 egg white
2 cups flour

Pinch of soda
¼ teaspoon salt
¼ teaspoon cinnamon
Nutmeats

Cream butter and sugar, add unbeaten egg yolk. Add other ingredients and spread over an 11-inch x 15-inch buttered cookie sheet. Beat egg white slightly and brush over top. Sprinkle with nuts and cinnamon. Bake at 300 degrees for 25 minutes. Turn off oven and let cookies remain in oven for a few minutes. Cut while warm in any desired shape.

Nellie C. DeVisser
Wayne County

MOTHER'S BUTTERSCOTCH SQUARES
German

2 cups flour
4 cups light brown sugar
½ teaspoon salt
2 teaspoons baking powder
1 cup butter or margarine,
   melted

4 eggs
2 teaspoons vanilla
1½ cups walnuts, chopped

Preheat oven to 350 degrees. In large bowl mix flour, sugar, salt and baking powder. Add melted butter and eggs. Blend thoroughly. Add vanilla and nuts and blend again. Grease and flour a 12-inch by 8-inch oblong pan and bake at 350 degrees approximately 20 minutes or until toothpick inserted is dry. When cool cut into squares.

Note: Delicious pick-me-ups and simple to make.

Marilyn K. Bruen
Putnam County

SMACHNYKY
Ukrainian

1 pound butter, softened
1 cup sugar
2 egg yolks
1 ounce fresh yeast

4 cups flour
Nutmeats, chopped
Egg white

Blend softened butter with sugar and beat, add yolks and beat some more. Add crumbled yeast and mix well. Add flour and put together lightly until all the flour is used up. Set in refrigerator for 20 minutes.
Form into any desired shape, round balls, crescents, logs, etc. Brush with beaten egg white and sprinkle with nuts. Bake in 375 degree oven about 20 minutes.

Ukrainian National Women's League
Monroe County

PARADISE PUFF PILLOWS
American Indian

2 cups flour	1 teaspoon salt
1½ teaspoons baking powder	2 teaspoons shortening

Mix together. Add enough lukewarm water to reduce sticking to hands. Knead the mixture until smooth. Divide into 2 loaves and roll each out to ⅛-inch thick. With knife, cut into 6-8 pieces.

To cook, drop pieces into extremely hot oil or shortening. Turn almost immediately. They will puff on the first turn. Remove from grease when golden brown. Pierce puff and fill with jam, jelly or honey.

Volunteer
Livingston County

HONEY NUT SQUARES
Pakistan

1 cup walnuts	¼ teaspoon cloves
¾ cup corn or whole wheat flakes	1 teaspoon baking powder
3 egg yolks	1 teaspoon orange rind, grated
¼ cup sugar	½ teaspoon lemon rind, grated
¼ teaspoon vanilla	3 egg whites
2 teaspoons water	½ cup honey
¼ teaspoon cinnamon	2 tablespoons water
	½ teaspoon lemon juice

Chop walnuts very fine. Crush cereal. Beat egg yolk until light colored. Add sugar, 2 tablespoons at a time and continue beating until thoroughly blended. Stir in vanilla, water, spices, baking powder, nuts, cereal, orange and lemon rind. Beat egg whites until peaks form. Fold into cereal mixture. Pour into greased 13-inch x 9-inch x 2-inch baking pan. Bake in moderate oven 350 degrees about 30 minutes. Cool in pan. Mix honey, water, lemon juice and pour over to glaze. Cut in squares.

Volunteer
Rockland County

SCOTCH SHORTBREAD
English

1 cup butter
½ cup confectioners' sugar

2 cups flour, sifted

Work the butter until smooth and creamy, then gradually work in confectioners' sugar again creaming thoroughly. Sift flour three times. Sift in flour a little at a time, mixing it in quickly and lightly. Chill dough about 30 minutes. Roll out shortbread ½-inch thick. Place on ungreased cookie sheet and prick with fork. Bake 5 minutes at 350 degrees, then reduce heat to 300 degrees and bake 20 to 25 minutes longer. Baked shortbreads should be light in color, not browned at all. Cut into pieces. These are rich, so make pieces small.

Note: They will seem slightly sweeter and notably mellower if seasoned for a week in a covered tin box and stored in a cool spot.

Mrs. James Kortz
Greene County

ROZHKI
(Filled Butter Horns)
Slavic

4 cups flour
1 cup butter
4 egg yolks, beaten
2 fresh yeast cakes

3 tablespoons sugar
½ teaspoon salt
½ pint thick sour cream

Blend flour and butter, combine eggs, yeast, sugar, salt, sour cream, combine the two mixtures lightly as for pie crust.
Form about 50 balls the size of walnuts but do not overwork dough. Place on cookie sheet, cover with wax paper and tea towel. Let stand in cool place or refrigerate overnight. Remove ½ hour before rolling. Using a floured rolling pin, roll each ball on lightly floured board to ¼-inch. Spread 1 teaspoon of desired filling and roll together and curve slightly to form horns. Bake on greased sheets at 350 degrees, after six minutes in oven, brush tops with 1 egg to which a little cream has been added. Finish baking about 15-20 minutes.

Mrs. Gabriel S. Kollar
Fulton County

CHOCOLATE MOUSSE PIE
French

8 ounces semisweet chocolate, squares or chips
1 tablespoon instant coffee
¼ cup boiling water
8 eggs, separated
⅔ cup granulated sugar
1 teaspoon vanilla or coffee liquor (optional)

⅛ teaspoon salt
1 cup heavy cream
¼ cup confectioners' sugar, sifted (optional)
1 teaspoon vanilla, (optional)

Preheat oven to 350 degrees. Place the chocolate in the top of a double boiler over hot, not boiling water. Dissolve the instant coffee in the boiling water and add to the chocolate. Cover and let stand over very low heat, stirring occasionally with a wire whisk. When the chocolate is almost melted, remove the top of the double boiler and whisk mixture until smooth. Meanwhile, beat the egg yolks until thick. Gradually beat in the sugar until the mixture is thick and lemon colored. Gradually beat the chocolate into the yolk mixture. Add in one teaspoon of vanilla. Beat the egg whites and salt until stiff but not dry. Stir ¼ of the whites into the chocolate. Fold in remaining whites gently. Dust a well-buttered 10-inch pie plate with sugar. Fill plate with ⅓ of chocolate mixture. Bake 25 minutes. Turn off heat and leave in oven for 5 minutes longer. Remove and cool. As it cools, the cooked mousse sinks in the middle to form a pie shell.
Meanwhile, cover and refrigerate the remaining uncooked mousse. Fill the cool shell with the chilled uncooked mousse. Chill 2-3 hours. Beat the cream, remaining vanilla and confectioners' sugar together until stiff. Spread over pie. May make a lattice pattern over pie. Serves 8.

Lynda Preiser
Delaware County

FRENCH CHOCOLATE WHISKEY CAKE
(Food Processor Recipe)
French

⅓ cup dark raisins
2 tablespoons whiskey
1 slice fresh white bread,
   broken into pieces
6 ounces blanched almonds
¾ cup butter or margarine,
   room temperature
¾ cup sugar

6 eggs, separated
½ pound semisweet chocolate,
   melted, cooled
2 teaspoons baking powder
Pinch salt
¼ teaspoon cream of tartar
Chocolate glaze

Soak raisins in whiskey. Using steel blade, process bread to fine crumbs, remove from bowl. Process almonds to fine powder, reserve. Using steel blade, process butter until fluffy. With machine running, gradually add sugar through feed tube. Process until fluffy. Add egg yolks, process until blended. Drain whiskey from raisins. Add whiskey, melted chocolate, bread crumbs, almonds and baking powder to bowl. Process until thoroughly blended. Transfer to a large mixing bowl. Heat oven to 350 degrees. Beat egg whites and salt with electric mixer until foamy. Add cream of tartar. Beat until stiff, do not let dry peaks form. Gently fold egg whites and raisins into chocolate mixture. Butter 9-inch springform pan. Line bottom with waxed paper or parchment paper. Butter and flour paper. Pour batter into pan. Bake until cake springs back when touched, 55-60 minutes. Cool on wire rack.

Make Chocolate Glaze — When cake has cooled, remove sides of springform pan. Invert cake onto serving plate. Remove bottom of springform pan and peel off paper.

Chocolate Glaze:
3 ounces sweet baking
   chocolate, melted, cooled
3 tablespoons butter or
   margarine, room temperature

¼ cup powdered sugar
2-3 tablespoons whiskey

Using plastic or steel blade, process all ingredients until smooth.

Spread top and sides with glaze. Refrigerate until glaze is firm.

Note: Cake can be decorated with whole or chopped almonds.

Carolyn Miller
Albany County

CHOCOLATE CAKE
(Yeast)
Irish

1 cup butter
2 cups, granulated sugar
3 eggs, separated
3 squares unsweetened
   chocolate, melted
1 cup cold milk
½ cake dry yeast

2½ cups cake flour
½ teaspoon salt
½ teaspoon baking soda
1½ teaspoons vanilla or
   teaspoon vanilla and ½
   teaspoon almond extract

Cream butter until light, gradually adding the sugar. Work in the well-beaten egg yolks, a little at a time, creaming and beating after each addition. Add 3 squares melted unsweetened chocolate, alternately with 1 cup milk, which has been mixed with ½ cake of dry yeast dissolved in ¼ cup lukewarm water. Blend thoroughly. Sift 2½ cups cake flour with salt 4 times, gradually add to first mixture. Mix well, then fold in stiffly beaten egg whites, cover the bowl and place in refrigerator overnight. In the morning stir in baking soda, dissolved in 3 tablespoons hot water—add vanilla or vanilla and almond. Blend thoroughly, turn batter into 2 buttered cake pans (9-inch x 9-inch x 3-inches) and bake in moderate oven—350 degrees for 40-45 minutes or until firm. Cool and cover with frosting.

Chocolate Frosting:
½ cup butter
2¾ cups confectioners' sugar
   (sifted 4 times)
2 egg yolks

2 squares unsweetened
   chocolate, melted, cinnamon
   or vanilla

Beat all ingredients together.

Jean M. Laux, R.N., E.T.
Broome County

OBEL KAGE
(Apple Cake)
Danish

½ cup butter or margarine
2 cups bread crumbs
1 tablespoon sugar

2½ cups applesauce
½ pint whipping cream
2 tablespoons sugar

Melt butter in a heavy frying pan. Add crumbs and sugar. Stir continually until bread crumbs are browned. Place prepared crumbs in serving dish alternately with layers of applesauce. Allow to harden in refrigerator. Serve cold with whipped cream sweetened with 2 tablespoons of sugar.

Agnes Christiansen
Yates County

ORANGE AND SPICE WALNUT CAKE
Greek

8 zwieback
1 pound walnuts
1½ cups sugar
7 eggs, separated
Rind of 1 orange, grated

½ teaspoon cinnamon
½ teaspoon nutmeg
1 teaspoon baking powder
Confectioners' sugar

Grind zwieback and walnuts in blender. Mix with sugar. Beat egg yolks until thick. Beat egg whites in large bowl until soft peaks form. Fold yolks into whites, alternately with zwieback mixture. Add orange rind, cinnamon, nutmeg and baking powder. Pour into well buttered 10 x 14 x 2-inch pan. Bake in 425 degree oven 15 minutes. Reduce temperature to 275 degrees. Bake 45 minutes longer. Cake is done when a cake tester inserted in center comes out clean. Cool cake in pan. Cut into squares. Sprinkle with confectioners' sugar. Serves 12-15.

Volunteer
Orange County

FRANKFURTERKRANZ
German

Cake:
½ cup margarine
¾ cup plus 1 tablespoon sugar
3 eggs
1 teaspoon lemon juice or ½
    teaspoon rum flavoring

1 cup plus 2 tablespoons flour
½ cup cornstarch
2 teaspoons baking powder

Bake in tube spring form pan, 375 degrees for 40-50 minutes.

Frosting:
2½ cups milk
⅓ cup plus 1 tablespoon sugar
5 tablespoons cornstarch
1 teaspoon vanilla or rum
    flavoring

3-4 drops yellow food coloring
4 tablespoons butter
4 tablespoons sugar

Bring to boiling point 2 cups milk. Mix thoroughly, sugar, cornstarch, flavoring and food coloring with ½ cup cold milk; add to hot mixture, stirring constantly until thickened. Remove from heat. Cream butter with sugar and add a spoonful at a time to cream mixture, whipping well.

Assemble and Decorate:
3 ounces sliced almonds
1 tablespoon butter

Maraschino cherries

Split cooled cake into three layers. Spread cooled cream mixture between layers, assemble layers on top of each other and spread remaining filling on sides and top. Toast almonds in butter and sugar and spread on top of cake, add maraschino cherries.

Elizabeth Geisler
Chautaugua County

PLUM CAKE
German

¾ cup butter
4 eggs
1 cup sugar
2 cups flour

2 cups pitted plums or plum
  halves
1 tablespoon cinnamon sugar

Cream butter and eggs, add sugar, flour and mix. Spread in a greased cake pan and slightly build up edges. Cover with plums overlapping slightly. Bake at 350 degrees about 45 minutes. Sprinkle with a tablespoon of cinnamon sugar after removing from oven.

Kristine Schug Stumpf
Orleans County

LOW-CHOLESTEROL EGGLESS APPLESAUCE CAKE
English

2 cups flour
1 cup sugar
2 teaspoons baking soda
2 teaspoons cinnamon
1 teaspoon salt

½ teaspoon nutmeg
¼ teaspoon cloves
1 pound can applesauce
½ cup margarine, melted
Raisins or nuts as desired

Sift together all dry ingredients. Add applesauce and melted margarine. Beat until blended. Stir in raisins or nuts or both if desired.
Bake in well-greased, floured 8 x 8-inch square pan at 350 degrees for 45-50 minutes.

Dorothy L. Gould
Oswego County

SWEDISH APPLE CAKE
Swedish

2 eggs	Pinch salt
1½ cups sugar	½ cup walnuts
1 cup flour	3 cups sliced apples
2 teaspoons baking powder	1 teaspoon vanilla

Beat eggs well, blend in sugar. Sift flour, baking powder, salt into egg and sugar mixture. Stir in walnuts, apples and vanilla.
Spread on a well-greased cookie sheet. Bake 350-375 degrees approximately 25-35 minutes. When cool cut into squares.

Volunteer
Otsego County

WELSH CAKES
Welsh

2 cups self-rising flour	½ cup sugar
½ teaspoon nutmeg	¾ cup raisins
2 ounces shortening	1 egg
2 ounces margarine	

Sift flour and nutmeg into medium size bowl. Add shortening and margarine and mix as in making pastry. Add sugar and raisins to this crumb-like mixture, then stir in the beaten egg. Add a little milk if necessary to make into a dough. Roll dough on cool floured surface to a good ¼-inch thickness and cut into rounds. Cook in electric frying pan at 350 degrees (no grease) until light golden color on both sides. Sprinkle with granulated sugar.

Julie Mariner
Steuben County

MAMOOL
Syrian

1½ pounds butter
  (no substitute)
2 cups sugar
½ teaspoon salt
3 tablespoons Orange Flower
  Water

4 cups flour
1 box (28 ounces) quick Cream
  of Wheat
½ cup hot milk

Nut filling:
1½ pounds walnuts, finely
  chopped
1 cup sugar

3 tablespoons Orange Flower
  Water

Syrup:
½ cup sugar   ½ cup hot water

Note: Ingredients may be purchased at Supermarkets.
Let butter get very soft, mix with sugar, add salt, flavoring, flour, Cream of Wheat. Mix well, add enough hot milk to hold the mixture together.

Spread a layer of mixture on bottom of greased pan (not the sides). Add layer of nut filling, then another layer of mixture on top. Cut into diamond shapes before baking. Bake in moderate oven (350 degrees) 35-45 minutes, until lightly browned. While still warm, pour syrup over the baked Mamool.
When cooled, separate pieces, dust with confectionary sugar.

Catherine Utter
Wayne County

FUNNEL CAKES
Pennsylvania Dutch

3 eggs
¼ cup sugar
2 cups milk

3-4 cups flour
½ teaspoon salt
2 teaspoons baking powder

Beat eggs and add sugar and milk. Sift half the flour, salt and baking powder together and add to milk and egg mixture. Beat the batter smooth and add only as much more flour as needed. Batter should be thin enough to run through a funnel. Drop from funnel into deep, hot fat (375 degrees). Spirals and endless intricate shapes can be made by swirling and criss-crossing while controlling the funnel spout with a finger. Serve hot with a sprinkle of powdered sugar.

Ms. Peggy Katz
Rockland County

BAVARIAN APPLE TORTE
German

½ cup margarine
⅓ cup sugar
¼ teaspoon vanilla
1 cup flour
1 8-ounce package cream
  cheese
¼ cup sugar

1 egg
½ teaspoon vanilla
⅓ cup sugar
½ teaspoon cinnamon
4 cups thin apple slices, peeled
¼ cup almonds, sliced

Preheat oven to 450 degrees. Cream margarine, sugar and vanilla. Blend in flour. Spread dough onto bottom and 2 inches high around sides of 9-inch springform pan. Combine softened cream cheese and sugar, mix well. Add egg and vanilla and mix well. Pour into pastry-lined pan. Combine sugar and cinnamon. Toss apples in sugar mixture. Spoon apple mixture over cream cheese layer. Sprinkle with nuts. Bake at 450 degrees for 10 minutes. Reduce oven temperature to 400 degrees, continue baking for 25 minutes. Cool before removing from pan. Serves 8-10.

Note: Apples that hold their shape, such as Empires or Ida Reds are the best to use. Excellent dessert for entertaining.

Mrs. Richard Roberts
Columbia County

PEPPORKAKOR
Scandinavian

1 cup shortening
1 cup granulated sugar
1 cup molasses
1 egg
2 tablespoons vinegar
5 cups flour

2-3 teaspoons ground ginger
1½ teaspoons baking soda
1 teaspoon ground cinnamon
1 teaspoon ground cloves
½ teaspoon salt

Frosting:
½ cup shortening
1 teaspoon vanilla
1 pound confectioners' sugar,
   sifted (3-4 cups)

3-4 tablespoons milk

Cream shortening and granulated sugar. Beat in molasses, egg, and vinegar. Stir flour with ginger, soda, cinnamon, cloves, and salt, blend with batter. Chill 3 hours. On lightly floured surface, roll dough to ⅛-inch thickness. Cut into usual shapes with assorted cookie cutters. Place 1-inch apart on greased cookie sheet. Bake at 375 degrees for 5-6 minutes. Cool slightly, remove cookies to racks and cool thoroughly.

Frosting
Blend shortening and vanilla with electric mixer. Gradually add powdered sugar, beat just until combined. Stir in milk. Insert small plain tip in pastry bag or cake decorator; fill with frosting. To decorate cookies, pipe frosting in straight or wavy lines, as desired. Yield: 5 dozen cookies.

Melodie A. Meara
Tioga County

OMA'S GERMAN CHOCOLATE TORTE
German

1 box Duncan Hines Swiss
  Chocolate Cake Mix
1 pound confectioners' sugar
6 teaspoons cocoa
2 egg yolks, room temperature

2 teaspoons vanilla
3 teaspoons Rum or Brandy
  (optional)
1 jar dark pitted cherries
  (strawberry jam may be
  substituted)

Prepare cake mix in two layers as directed on box.
Cream butter with confectioners' sugar, adding a spoon at a time, stir in 3 teaspoons of cocoa, egg yolks, vanilla and Rum for light butter cream frosting. Remove half of the frosting to a separate bowl and add remaining 3 teaspoons cocoa for darker butter cream. Reserve a little of both for decorating.
Spread light frosting on layers.
Heat cherries and thicken with cornstarch, cool and spread on layers (or use the jam).
Place one layer on top of the other and frost with darker cream. Using a cake decorator bag, pipe on remainder of both color frostings in a design of your choice.

Hannah Turk
Essex County

STRAWBERRY MERINGUE TORTE
French

3 egg whites
½ teaspoon baking powder
1 cup sugar
½ cup pecans, chopped
10 Saltine crackers (squares),
  crushed

1 cup heavy cream
2 tablespoons sugar
1 quart strawberries, cleaned,
  hulled and sliced in half

Preheat oven to 350 degrees. Grease 9-inch pie plate. Beat egg whites, baking powder and sugar until whites are stiff, not dry. Fold in nuts and crackers. Put in pie plate and bake at 350 degrees for 30 minutes. Cool at room temperature. Fill with fresh fruit (unsweetened). Whip heavy cream, adding 2 tablespoons sugar, until stiff. Cover fruit completely and chill for several hours. Serves 6-8.

Note: This is our favorite way to enjoy Oswego County strawberries.

Marcia B. Madden
Oswego County

ITALIAN TORTI
Italian

Mix:

4 cups flour	2 sticks of margarine, softened
½ teaspoon salt	2 teaspoons Anise extract
1½ cups sugar	½ cup glazed red cherries
4 teaspoons baking powder	¼ cup walnuts, ground
4 eggs, medium, beaten	(optional)
½ cup milk	

Icing:

1 cup confectioners' sugar	1 teaspoon Anise extract
1 tablespoon margarine, softened	2 tablespoons milk

Preheat oven at 350 degrees. Line baking sheet with Reynolds Wrap. Mix all ingredients together, blend by hand. Roll mixture on a floured board in a shape of a long loaf of bread. This makes four medium loaves of cookie bread. Bake for 25 to 30 minutes. When done let the cookie bread cool, and spread the icing on. Slice as needed.

Rose DelVecchio
Greene County

FRUIT TORTE
German

¾ cup flour
½ teaspoon baking soda
⅓ cup sugar
1 egg
1 teaspoon vanilla

5 tablespoons butter
1 large can fruit, drained
Juice from fruit
Cornstarch

Sift flour with baking soda in bowl. Separate flour mixture with spoon to make hole in center, pour in sugar, egg and vanilla and mix lightly. Cut butter in small pieces, add to mixture. Knead together until well mixed. (If too soft, add a little flour).
Butter a jelly roll pan. With spoon spread dough in pan, leaving a high edge on sides. Bake 20-25 minutes, 325-350 degrees. Cool, spread drained fruit over crust (any kind).
Mix about 1½ tablespoons of cornstarch in ¼ cup of fruit juice to make a thin paste. Heat remaining juice to boiling, slowly pour in cornstarch mixture, stir until thickened. Remove from heat immediately. Cool. Pour over fruit.
Serve cold with whipped cream.

Volunteer
Jefferson County

NUT TORTE
German

6 eggs
½ pound nuts, ground

1 cup sugar

Beat egg whites until they are stiff. In mixing bowl beat egg yolks and sugar until creamy. Fold in beaten egg whites and ground nuts. Bake in springform, lined with wax paper, in 350 degree oven for 40 minutes. Let cool before frosting or cutting. Cut cake in half. Fill and frost with whipped cream. Cake cuts best if baked a day before filling.

Mrs. Marie Kruse
Tioga County

HAZELNUT TORTE
German

4 eggs
¾ cup sugar
1 cup Hazelnuts (also called
  Filberts), finely ground
2 tablespoons all-purpose flour,
  sifted

2½ teaspoons baking powder
Confectioners' sugar
Sweetened whipped cream

Preheat oven to 350 degrees. Grease 2 8-inch pans and line with wax paper or foil. Place eggs and sugar in blender and process at low speed until blended. Turn control to high, remove cover and add nuts, flour and baking powder (which have been previously mixed together). Blend 2-3 minutes—nuts will be very finely ground. Pour in pans, bake 20 minutes. Cool 10 minutes. Invert and remove from pans. Put sifted confectioners' sugar on each. Spread sweetened whipped cream between layers and serve with a small amount of cream spread on top.

Note: Hazelnuts or Filberts may be found in a Health Food Store.

Carolyn Foster
Ontario County

Entrées

The Chenango Canal
The Thruway of Yesterday

The methods and means of transportation in this State progressed from nothing more than original crude Indian trails to narrow dirt paths and from there to privately owned log roads and turnpikes, statebuilt canals, railroad lines and finally to State and County networks of roads and highways.

The most important and far reaching step in this development was the introduction of the far-flung canal system of New York State in the early nineteenth century. This system at its peak included more than 16 canals totalling nearly 750 miles and reaching into every section of the Empire State. Although New York State was not the first State to build canals, its Erie Canal was the longest artifical water-way of its period in America.

Far more important, however, is the fact that its entire canal system was built under the supervision of lawyers, judges and others who had no experience or training in the field of canal construction and by immigrant laborers who used it as a means to move westward. This situation is well illustrated by the experience of Carvas White, an American, who went to England and walked 1,000 miles along her canals in order to observe how they were built; with this information and practical ingenuity, that has built all aspects of America, New York created between 1817 and1860 its first State "highway" system.

BEEF STRIPS ORIENTAL
Oriental

1 pound round steak, ¾-inch thick	1 cup celery, sliced
Oil	2 cups mushroom halves
1 cup water	¼ cup cold water
2 tablespoons soy sauce	2 tablespoons cornstarch
1 garlic clove, minced	½ cup Parmesan cheese, grated
1 cup carrots, sliced	Hot cooked rice

Cut meat into strips ¼-inch wide and 3-4 inches long. Brown meat in oil, drain. Add water, soy sauce and garlic. Cover, simmer 45 minutes. Add vegetables, cover and continue cooking 15-20 minutes. Combine cornstarch and water, stirring until well blended. Gradually add cornstarch mixture to hot meat and vegetables, stirring constantly until mixture boils and thickens. Remove from heat, stir in cheese. Serve over rice. Serves 4.

Mary Aubel
Ulster County

FLEMISH BEEF
Flemish

1¼ pounds flank steak	2 teaspoons sugar
3 tablespoons butter	1 tablespoon vinegar
2 onions, thinly sliced	1 teaspoon salt
3 tablespoons flour	Black pepper, freshly ground
2 cups beer	1 slice white bread, crusts
1 bay leaf	removed
1 teaspoon thyme	1 tablespoon prepared (Dijon
1 sprig parsley	type) mustard

Cut flank steak into pieces and brown lightly in butter over high heat. Remove meat from pan. Sauté the onions in the same butter. Add the flour and cook until light brown. Gradually add the beer, stirring constantly until the sauce is thickened and smooth. Add the meat, bay leaf, thyme, parsley, sugar, vinegar, salt and pepper. Cover the pan and let the meat simmer slowly for 1 hour. Spread the slice of bread with mustard and place the bread in the pan. Simmer for 1 hour more.

Denise Lupton
Ontario County

BEEF IN BEER
German

¼ cup oil
5 medium onions, sliced
2 cloves garlic
3 pounds beef chuck or rump
   cut into 1-inch cubes

¼ cup flour
2½ cups beer
2 teaspoons parsley flakes
2 bay leaves
½ teaspoon thyme

In a large, heavy kettle heat the oil. Sauté the onion and garlic. Dust the cubes of beef with flour and brown in the oil. Lower the heat and add the beer, parsley, bay leaves and thyme. Simmer, closely covered, stirring occasionally, for two hours or until beef is tender.

Note: Especially good over homemade noodles or Spatzle.

Mrs. Arnold Duszynski
Cattaraugus County

BEEF BOURGUIGNON
French

3-4 medium sized onions
2 tablespoons bacon drippings
2 pounds lean beef (sirloin tip
   or chuck)
1½ tablespoons flour
Marjoram

Thyme
Salt and pepper
½ cup beef bouillon
1 cup dry New York State
   Burgundy
½-¾ pound fresh mushrooms

Slice onions and fry in bacon drippings until brown, using a heavy skillet. Remove to a separate dish. Cut beef into 1-inch cubes and sauté in drippings. When beef cubes are browned on all sides, sprinkle them with 1½ tablespoons of flour, adding a generous pinch each of salt, pepper, marjoram and thyme. Add ½ cup of bouillon and the cup of Burgundy to skillet. Let mixture simmer as slowly as possible for 3¼ hours. The liquid may cook away some, so add a little more bouillon and wine (in proportion of 1 part stock to 2 parts wine). After mixture has cooked 3¼ hours, return the browned onions to the skillet, and then add the fresh, sliced mushrooms. Stir everything together and cook for ¾ of an hour (or even 1 hour longer). Sauce should be thick and dark brown.

Serve with rice, crusty French bread, a tossed salad, and a bottle of good Burgundy. Follow with a light dessert. Serves 6-8.

William Gerber
Erie County

RHEINISCHER SAUERBRATEN
(RHINELAND MARINATED POT ROAST)
German

5 pounds rump of beef
Bacon or salt pork for larding
Salt
3 cups white vinegar
3 cups water
1 large onion, sliced
2 bay leaves
8 cloves
8 peppercorns
1 tablespoon pickling spices
1 large carrot, scraped and
　sliced

4 slices bacon and 2
　tablespoons butter or 5
　tablespoons bacon fat, kidney
　fat or beef drippings
2 large onions, sliced
1 bay leaf
6 cloves
2 tablespoons butter
3 tablespoons flour
2 tablespoons sugar
Lemon juice to taste
½ cup white raisins, soaked in
　warm water

Rump should be well larded with thin matchstick strips of bacon or salt pork. This can be done by you or your butcher. Tie meat firmly with string in several places so it will be easy to turn without piercing, and will hold its shape. Rub well with salt on all sides and place in deep closefitting glass or earthenware bowl. Combine vinegar and water and add onion, bay leaves, cloves, peppercorns, pickling spices and carrot. Bring to a boil and simmer 5 minutes. Cool marinade and pour over beef. The meat should be completely covered by marinade, if it is not, add equal amounts of water and vinegar until it is. Cover and place in refrigerator for 3-5 days, the longer it stands, the more piquant the roast will be, so adjust time to suit your own taste. Turn meat in marinade 2-3 times each day, using the string as a handle. Remove meat from marinade. Strain marinade and reserve. Dry meat thoroughly on all sides with plenty of paper toweling. (The meat will not brown properly if it is wet.)

Dice bacon and fry it slowly in butter in a 5-quart Dutch oven or casserole. When fat is hot, add meat and brown slowly. Using the string as a handle, turn so meat is well seared and golden brown on all sides. This should take about 15 minutes. Remove browned meat and add sliced onions to hot fat. Fry, stirring from time to time, until onions are deep golden brown, but not black.

Return meat to pot, placing it on top of onions; add marinade until it reaches about halfway up sides of meat. Add bay leaf, and cloves (not those used in marinade). Bring marinade to a boil, cover pot tightly, reduce heat and simmer very, very slowly but steadily for 3½-4 hours, turning meat two or three times during cooking. Add more marinade to pot, if needed. The meat is done when it can be pierced easily with a long-pronged fork or skewer.

Rheinischer Sauerbraten (continued)

Remove meat to a heated platter and strain gravy. Skim off excess fat and return gravy to pot. Melt butter in saucepan, (2 tablespoons), and when hot, stir in flour and sugar. Cook over very low heat, stirring constantly until sugar mixture turns a deep caramel color. Be very careful doing this as sugar burns all at once and, if it becomes black, you will have to start this part of the operation all over again.

Add the sugar-flour to the hot gravy and stir through briskly with a wire whisk. Season with lemon juice, to taste, gravy should have a mild sweet-sour flavor. Add raisins which have been soaked and drained. Return meat to pot, cover and simmer 10 minutes. If sauce becomes too thick, add a little more marinade.

Slice meat and arrange on a heated platter and mask with a little gravy, serving the rest in a heated sauceboat.

Mrs. Joseph D. Stephen, Jr.
Clinton County

STEAK DIANE
French

1 filet mignon (2-3 ounce slices,
    1-inch thick)
1½ ounces cognac
1 ounce Burgundy wine

2 tablespoons mushrooms,
    sliced
Salt and pepper to taste

Heat one piece of butter in frying pan, add the filet mignons, season with salt and pepper. When done to taste add the cognac and flame. Add the Burgundy wine and stir well. Add the mushrooms, stir again and serve with a green salad and fluffy rice.

Note: To compliment, a good Burgundy wine.

Volunteer
Greene County

BOEUF RAGOUT
French

3 pounds beef, cut into cubes
1 can tomatoes (1 pound)
2 medium onions, sliced
½ teaspoon ground ginger

⅓ cup red wine vinegar
½ cup dark molasses
6-8 carrots, sliced
½ cup raisins

In a large kettle, place the beef, tomatoes, onions, ginger, vinegar and molasses. Add a little water if necessary and simmer until beef is tender (about 2 hours). Add carrots, raisins and simmer until carrots are tender. Serve over hot rice. Serves 6.

Doris Greeno
Warren County

LEON'S CHINESE STEAK WITH GARLIC
Chinese

1 pound boneless sirloin or
  bottom round
2 tablespoons soy sauce
1 tablespoon hoisin sauce (or
  extra soy sauce, if hoisin is
  not available)

2 tablespoons dry sherry
1½ teaspoons sugar
4 cloves garlic, peeled and
  sliced (more if you are a
  garlic lover)
3 tablespoons oil

Cut sirloin against the grain into slices 2-inches long by 1-inch wide by ¼-inch thick. Set on platter exposing one side of each piece. Cover with mixture of soy sauce, hoisin sauce, and sherry. Sprinkle with sugar. Arrange thin garlic slices over steak. Marinate 1 hour or more at room temperature.

Set wok over highest heat for 30 seconds, swirl in oil, heat to almost smoking, remove beef from marinade with slotted spoon. Reserve marinade. Stir-fry steak quickly for 2 minutes. After 1½ minutes, pour remaining marinade over steak so that it finishes cooking in marinade. Serve at once. Serves 4.

Note: Serve with plain rice, and a mixed vegetable salad.

Arlene Kiersz
Cattaraugus County

ROULADEN
German

6 slices top round steak,
  ½-inch thick
6 teaspoons hot mustard
¼ cup onion, finely chopped
6 slices lean bacon, chopped
3 dill pickles, rinsed in cold
  water and halved, lengthwise
3 tablespoons lard

1 cup water
1 cup red wine
1 cup celery, chopped
¼ cup leeks, thinly sliced
3 sprigs parsley
1 teaspoon salt
1 tablespoon butter
2 tablespoons flour

Trim the meat of all fat and pound to ¼-inch. Spread each slice with 1 tablespoon mustard, sprinkle with 2 teaspoons chopped onion and 1 slice bacon, chopped. Sprinkle lightly with salt and pepper. Place a pickle half across the meat at the narrow end. Roll the meat around the pickle (as in a jelly-roll). Secure both ends with string or a small skewer. Melt the lard over moderate heat in an iron skillet until it sputters. Evenly brown the meat in the hot lard. Remove from pan. Add the water and wine and bring to a boil, stirring to remove loose particles from pan. Add celery, leeks, parsley and salt. Return beef rolls to the skillet. Cover and simmer until meat is tender (approximately one hour). Keep meat on a heated platter covered with foil while making sauce.

Using a fine sieve, strain liquid, pressing vegetables to remove juice. Return the liquid to the skillet and boil until reduced to 2 cups. Melt the butter in a small saucepan. Sprinkle with the flour. Cook over low heat, stirring, until flour is golden. Gradually add cooking liquid to the butter mixture, beating with a wire whisk until the sauce is smooth and thick. Return the sauce and beef rolls to the skillet and simmer just until heated through. Serve Rouladen on a heated platter with the sauce poured over the top.

For a special treat, sauce may be thickened with one cup of sour cream in place of the butter and flour.

Marilyn Foster
Dutchess County

SWEET POTATO AND PRUNE TZIMMES
Jewish

1½ pounds (1 box) prunes
3 pounds brisket of beef
Salt and pepper to taste
6 medium sweet potatoes,
  pared and cut

½ cup sugar
1½ tablespoons lemon juice

Combine prunes, meat and enough water to cover in a heavy pot. Season to taste. Bring to a boil and simmer over very low heat until meat is almost tender (approximately 1½ hours). Remove meat and prunes from gravy and add pared sweet potatoes. Place potatoes and prunes on top of meat. Sprinkle with sugar and lemon juice. Cover and bake 300 degrees until potatoes and meat brown (approximately 1 hour). Serves 6.

Note: Traditional Jewish New Years dish to usher in a sweet year.

Mrs. Shirley Weinman
Chenango County

GOULASH
Hungarian

1 pound stewing meat
1 teaspoon paprika
6 ounces onions, chopped
1 teaspoon caraway seed

2 ounces lard
1 clove garlic
1 teaspoon tomato purée
1 tablespoon flour

Cut meat in cubes and wash well. Fry onions in lard till they begin to brown. Stir in paprika; sprinkle salt on meat and place in pan with onions and paprika, adding a little water, garlic, caraway seed and tomato purée. Stew slowly with lid on until tender, adding a little water during cooking, if necessary. When cooked, sprinkle with flour and stir; add more water to cover meat; bring to boil and simmer for a few minutes. Serve with spaghetti, rice or potatoes. Serves 4.

Volunteer
Broome County

PEPPER STEAK—FRENCH STYLE
French

10 ounce sirloin steak	1½ ounces red wine
Mustard	Bordelaise
1 ounce cognac	2 ounces heavy cream
1 tablespoon whole green peppercorns	Salt to taste

Heat one piece of butter in a frying pan and cook the steak, turn and spread with mustard. Do the same on the other side. When steak is done to taste, add the cognac and flame. Sprinkle with the green pepper, add the red wine, bordelaise sauce with mushrooms, reduce and add the cream. Stir well, add salt to taste and serve.

Volunteer
Genesee County

ITALIAN MEAT AND PEPPERS
Italian

1½ pounds beef	½ cup boiling water
1½ pounds veal	6 green peppers, sliced thin
4 onions, chopped	4 tomatoes, sliced
3 tablespoons oil	2 cloves garlic, chopped
2 teaspoons salt	¼ teaspoon oregano
½ teaspoon pepper	Few sprigs parsley

Cut beef and veal into cubes, chop onions fine, heat oil in Dutch oven. Add meat and onions and cook over a medium heat until all are browned. Now season with salt and pepper and add boiling water, cover and cook over a low heat for about 1½ hours or until meat is tender. Add peppers, tomatoes, garlic, oregano and parsley. Bake at 375 degrees, toss vegetables into meat, cover and bake 20 minutes. Remove cover and cook 20 minutes longer.

Mrs. Mitchell Myzal
Fulton County

NORWEGIAN MEATBALLS
Scandinavian

1½ pounds round steak
½ pound lean pork
½ pound lean veal
2 eggs
¾ cup light cream
1 tablespoon onion, minced
1¼ teaspoons salt

¼ teaspoon pepper
1 teaspoon ginger
½ teaspoon cloves
¾ cup flour
1 teaspoon baking powder
4 tablespoons butter

Grind beef, pork and veal together *two* times and place in large bowl of electric mixer. In separate bowl, beat the eggs to blend well. Add cream and minced onion, combine with meat. Stir together salt, pepper, ginger, cloves, flour and baking powder and blend into meat mixture. Mix well in electric mixer for 15 minutes at medium low speed. Form into small meatballs (walnut size). Brown lightly in melted butter. Add water to cover and simmer for 1½ hours. Thicken for gravy. For added richness, add ½ cup sour cream.

Aleda Souders
Chenango County

GOLOMKI
Polish

2 heads savoy cabbage
2 pounds hamburg
1 package dried onion soup
Sprig of parsley
Salt and pepper to taste
2 eggs

2 cups cooked rice
1 can (8 ounces) tomato sauce
2 cans (10½-ounces) tomato soup
Garlic salt

Preheat oven to 400 degrees. Split and parboil cabbage, put in mix of hamburg, dried onion soup, parsley, salt and pepper, eggs, cooked rice, tomato sauce and wrap up. Use large broiler pan (10 x 13-inch) and line with golomki and stick extra cabbage on side. Pour 2 cans of tomato soup and 1½-cans water over golomki. Sprinkle with garlic salt. Cover the pan. Start baking at 400 degrees and then turn to 325 degrees for 1 hour. It is done when hamburg is hardened. Yield: 15-18.

Joan M. Hughes
Schenectady County

WEST INDIAN MEAT PATTIES
West Indian

Filling:
1 pound ground beef
1 medium onion
1 teaspoon ground hot pepper
1 teaspoon of homemade
   seasoning (mix salt, pepper
   and paprika together)
2 cloves garlic, minced
1 tablespoon vinegar
2½ cups tomatoes, (canned)
1 tablespoon tomato paste

3 tablespoons shortening,
   melted
1 sprig of thyme or pinch of
   ground thyme
2 tablespoons of parsley,
   chopped
2 tablespoons green peppers,
   chopped
2 tablespoons of stuffed olives,
   chopped

Crust:
4 cups flour
1 teaspoon salt
½ cup shortening

Water enough to make dough
   easy to handle

Filling—Combine all ingredients with the ground beef meat. Place in skillet, cover and steam until meat is tender. Mix flour and water to smooth liquid. Flour mixture—3 tablespoons of flour and 5 tablespoons of water. Add water slowly. Add filling to the mixture. Cook until thick. Remove from heat and allow to cool.

Crust—Sift flour and salt together until mixture resembles coarse corn meal. Add water and continue to cut into mixture until mixture leaves the bowl. Roll out, cut into 3-3½-inch circles. Fill with meat filling. Turn over and press the edges firmly together. Be sure to keep the filling close to the center of the circle. Fry in boiling fat or oil for approximately 15 minutes. Let brown and place on a napkin to allow the extra fat to be absorbed. Yield: 24 medium sized patties.

Mrs. Dorothy E. Anderson
Orange County

MEXICAN CHILI
Mexican

4 pounds stew-meat or
hamburger, coarsely ground
1 teaspoon salt
¼-½ teaspoon pepper
1 large onion, chopped
1 teaspoon garlic powder
2 teaspoons ground cumin
4-6 teaspoons chili powder
(may add more if desired,
depends how hot you like it)

¾ cup flour
2 16-ounce cans tomatoes,
chopped
2 6-ounce cans tomato paste
8 cups water (more if
necessary)

Brown meat in large pot or Dutch oven. (I use a roasting pan). Add salt, pepper, chopped onion, garlic powder, cumin, chili powder and flour. Stir often. Add tomatoes, tomato paste and water. If too thick you may add more water. Simmer on low heat for 3-4 hours before serving. You may add kidney beans if desired. Serve with salad, corn chips, or cornbread for a complete meal. Leftovers may be frozen for later use.

Note: This is a basic recipe for enchilada casserole and corn chips casserole.

Peggy D. Sandstrom
Chautauqua County

TÖLTÖTT KÁPOSZTA
Hungarian

1 large head cabbage
1½ pounds of beef, ground
2 tablespoons salt
1 tablespoon paprika
1 teaspoon black pepper

¼ pound rice, washed well
1 large onion, minced
3 tablespoons shortening
1 small can sauerkraut
1 #2 can tomato juice

Core cabbage and place in enough boiling salted water to cover. With a fork in one hand and a knife in the other keep cutting off the leaves as they become wilted. Drain. Trim thick center vein of each cabbage leaf. Brown onion in shortening. Add meat, seasonings and rice; mix well. Place a tablespoon of filling on each cabbage leaf and roll and tuck in ends. Place in pot and cover two-thirds full with water, arrange sauerkraut on top, add tomato juice. Cover and cook slowly for about 1½ hours or until rice is tender. Serves 6-8.

Irene H. Ferenczy
Schoharie County

HAMBURGER POTATO ROLL
English

1 tablespoon drippings
1 medium onion, chopped
1 small clove garlic, crushed
1 pound ground chuck beef
1 egg, lightly beaten
2 slices bread, crusts removed
Water
1 teaspoon salt
¼ teaspoon oregano, rosemary
   or basil

Black pepper to taste, finely
   ground
2 tablespoons dry bread
   crumbs
2 cups mashed potato,
   seasoned
1 tablespoon parsley or green
   pepper, minced (optional)
3 strips bacon (optional)

Preheat oven to moderate 350 degrees. Heat the drippings, add the onion, garlic and sauté until the onion is transparent. Remove to a mixing bowl and add the ground beef. Add the egg. Soften the bread in water, press out the excess water and add bread to the meat. Add salt, oregano and pepper. Mix thoroughly. Sprinkle a piece of waxed paper with crumbs. Press the meat out on the crumbs to make a rectangle about one half-inch thick. Beat the mashed potatoes with the parsley and spread on top of the meat. (If leftover potato is used, reheat it in a double boiler before spreading.) Use the waxed paper as an aid, roll the meat and potatoes, jelly-roll fashion, and place the bacon on top or brush with additional drippings; baste at least once during baking. Bake about one hour and serve with a brown sauce made from the pan drippings, or with mushrooms, tomato or other sauce.

Fred Rivers
Seneca County

ITALIAN STYLE STUFFED EGGPLANT
Italian

4 medium eggplants (about
  1 pound each) unpared
8 ounces lean ground beef
1 clove garlic, finely chopped
½ cup onion, finely chopped
2 tablespoons olive oil
¼ cup Italian parsley, snipped
1 teaspoon salt
1 teaspoon dried sweet basil
¼ teaspoon black pepper

4 ounces (¾ cup) proscuitto
  (Italian ham)
½ cup dry bread crumbs
¼ cup Parmesan cheese, grated
2 tablespoons water
2 tablespoons olive oil
2 medium ripe tomatoes,
  quartered
Salt and pepper to taste

Half eggplant and scoop out pulp leaving ¼-inch shell. Cut pulp in ¾-inch pieces. Heat oven to 350 degrees. Cook and stir in 2 tablespoons of oil, beef, onion and garlic 5 minutes. Stir in eggplant pulp, parsley, 1 teaspoon salt, the basil and ⅛ teaspoon pepper. Cook and stir until eggplant is barely tender (7-10 minutes). Remove from heat. Stir in Italian ham, bread crumbs and cheese. Spoon mixture into eggplant shells, packing firmly. Arrange on ungreased baking pan. Pour 2 tablespoons water and 2 tablespoons oil into bottom of pan. Bake uncovered 35 minutes. Arrange tomato quarters on stuffed eggplant and bake 10 minutes more. Serve in shells.

Mary-Ellen Castiglione
Ulster County

SARMA
Greek

30-50 grape leaves
½ cup rice (minute or regular)
2 pounds ground beef
1 medium onion, chopped
1 clove garlic, chopped

Dash salt
Dash red pepper
1 8-ounce can tomato sauce
2 whole cloves garlic

Rinse salt from leaves before using. Put grape leaves in hot, boiling water and remove from stove and let them stand five minutes or until tender. Wash rice two times. Combine rice, meat, chopped onion, chopped garlic, red pepper and salt. Add ¾ can of tomato sauce (reserve rest for later). Mix together well. Place one tablespoon of mixture inside of tender, grape leaf. Fold sides of leaf to center and roll up like a jelly roll. It should be long and narrow when finished. Put in a 4-quart pan: ¼ can tomato sauce and two cups water, two cloves (whole) garlic and filled grape leaves. Cook until meat and rice are done. When done, sprinkle with 2 tablespoons lemon juice.

E. Wm. Miller
Erie County

TUNISIAN LAMB
Tunisia

1 tablespoon salad oil
1 pound boned lamb
1 medium onion, chopped
2 cups beef broth
½ teaspoon cinnamon
¼ teaspoon salt
¼ teaspoon pepper
¼ teaspoon ground ginger

2 medium apples, peeled, cored
  and diced
1 16-ounce can sweet potatoes,
  drained
6 pitted prunes, halved
4 lemon slices
3 tablespoons honey

In a 12-inch skillet over medium temperature, heat salad oil. Add lamb and onion and brown well on all sides, stirring occasionally. Pour off any drippings. Add broth, cinnamon, salt, pepper and ginger. Heat to boiling. Reduce heat, cover and simmer for 1 hour, 15 minutes. Add apples, sweet potatoes, prunes, lemon and honey. Cook, uncovered, for 15 minutes more, or until the apples are tender, stirring occasionally. Serves 4.

Nancy Simmonds
Cayuga County

SKILLET LAMB CHOPS AND PILAF
Greek

2 chicken bouillon cubes
1¼ cups water
1 tablespoon butter
1 garlic clove, finely minced
4 shoulder lamb chops

½ cup long-grain rice
1 teaspoon salt
Juice of ½ fresh lemon
Parsley
Pepper to taste

Dissolve bouillon cubes in boiling water. Set aside. Melt butter in heavy skillet. Sauté garlic. Quickly sear chops over high heat. Pour in bouillon. Pour rice around chops. Add salt. Sprinkle with lemon, parsley and pepper. Bring to boil. Cover. Simmer 25-30 minutes or until rice is tender and liquid is absorbed. Let stand, covered, 5 minutes before serving. Serves 2-4.

Volunteer
Cayuga County

SHISH KEBABS
Pakistan

1 teaspoon curry powder
1½ tablespoons salt
3 bay leaves
6-8 peppercorns
2 tablespoons onion, grated
1 large clove garlic, crushed
¼ cup lemon juice
¼ cup dry red wine

⅓ cup olive oil
2 pounds tender lamb, cut in
    1½-inch cubes
Green pepper squares
Small white onions, partially
    cooked
Tomato wedges
Mushroom caps

Combine seasonings, lemon juice, dry red wine and olive oil in bowl. Place lamb, green peppers and onions in mixture and allow to marinate 4-12 hours. Drain meat and vegetables, reserve marinade. Alternately place marinated meat, green peppers, onions, tomatoes and mushroom caps on skewers. Line broiler tray with foil. Place kebabs on foil and brush with marinade. Broil 20-30 minutes turning and basting often until kebabs are browned on all sides. Or cook on charcoal broiler outdoors. Serves 6.

Volunteer
Jefferson County

MOUSSAKA
Greek

2 1-pound eggplants
3 tablespoons salt
2 cups flour
½ cup cooking oil
¼ pound butter
3 cloves garlic
2 medium onions, chopped
2 pounds lamb, ground
½ teaspoon oregano

¼ teaspoon cinnamon
Freshly ground black pepper
½ cup red wine
3 tablespoons parsley, chopped
1 large can tomatoes, drained
   and chopped
½ cup bread crumbs
¼ cup fresh mushrooms
4 ounces Parmesan cheese

Slice ½-inch wide strips of peel vertically from eggplants. Slice eggplants crossways in ½-inch widths. Soak in salted pot of water 30 minutes. Dry with paper towels, coat with flour, brown quickly in oil on both sides. Drain on paper towels. Melt butter in large skillet, add crushed garlic, onions and brown. Next add lamb, brown slowly, then add spices, wine, tomatoes, and mushrooms. Bring to boil and let simmer 15 minutes. Use a 14 x 10-inch baking dish or a deep round dutch oven. Butter bottom, cover with ½ the bread crumbs. Next place a layer of eggplant slices over this. Cover with about ⅓ of the meat mixture and then ⅓ of the cheese. Then repeat bread crumbs, eggplant, meat, and cheese, again until all ingredients are used. Save some of the cheese and bread crumbs for later. Lastly pour the Bechamel sauce over the top, spread evenly and sprinkle with the cheese and breadcrumbs. Bake in preheated oven at 350 degrees for 45 minutes.

Bechamel Sauce:
3 tablespoons butter
¼ cup flour
3 cups milk
¼ teaspoon nutmeg

¼ teaspoon garlic salt
Fresh ground pepper
4 egg yolks

Melt butter, blend in flour slowly, over low heat for one minute. Add the milk slowly using wire whisk, make smooth thick sauce. Be patient, as it takes a while to thicken. Season with salt, pepper and nutmeg. Keep hot. Beat egg yolks in bowl lightly. Add a few tablespoons of the hot sauce and whip with wire whisk, then add egg yolk mixture to remaining sauce, mixing well.

Dr. James Adams
Chemung County

PASTELILLOS
(Meat Turnovers)
Spanish

1 teaspoon salt
½ teaspoon baking powder
3 cups flour
½ cup shortening
⅓ cup milk
2 pounds pork butt
1 medium onion
½ green pepper
1 tomato or 1 8-ounce can
  stewed tomatoes or tomato
  sauce

2 cloves garlic
2 teaspoons salt
⅛ teaspoon black pepper
¼ teaspoon oregano
1 teaspoon stuffed olives,
  chopped
1 teaspoon capers
2 cups oil, or shortening for
  deep fat frying

In large bowl mix salt and baking powder. Cut in shortening with pastry cutter. Add milk, blend with a fork to make a soft dough (use more liquid if needed). Set aside. Coarsely grind pork butt, brown the pork in a dutch oven. Mince onion, green pepper, tomato and garlic (or grind in blender). Add to browned pork, add olives and capers. Cook over medium heat until done (about 30 minutes). Set aside to cool, separate dough into 1½-inch diameter balls. Roll out into 6-inch turnovers on a lightly floured surface. Drain filling with slotted spoon and place about 1 tablespoon of filling in center of turnover. Fold and seal edges with a fork. (Can be frozen at this point.) Fry in 2 cups hot oil or shortening until golden, drain and serve immediately. Yield: 24-36.

Note: Popular at Christmas in Puerto Rico. Serve with a vegetable and salad or excellent as an appetizer when made smaller.

Margaret Dafeldeeker
Schoharie County

KIELBASA W POLSKIM SOSIE
(Sausage in Polish Sauce)
Polish

2 onions, sliced
3 tablespoons butter or
  margarine
1 ring Polish sausage
  (about 1½ pounds)
1½ cups bouillon or meat broth
12 ounces beer

2 tablespoons flour
1 tablespoon vinegar
2 teaspoons brown sugar
¾ teaspoon salt
¼ teaspoon pepper
4-6 boiled potatoes

Sauté onion in 2 tablespoons butter until golden. Add sausage, bouillon, and beer. Simmer 20 minutes. Blend flour into remaining 1 tablespoon butter. Stir into broth. Add vinegar, brown sugar, salt, and pepper. Add potatoes. Cook over medium heat 10-15 minutes. Slice sausage into 2-inch chunks to serve.

Mrs. Betty J. Grinnell
Cortland County

PORK BUUITO
Mexican

1-2 pounds lean pork, cut into
  1-inch cubes
2-3 10-ounce cans peeled
  tomatoes
1 tablespoon cumin
2 cloves garlic
¼ teaspoon dry red pepper
3 stalks celery, chopped

1 onion, chopped
2-3 Jalapaneo peppers, without
  seeds
Floured tortillas
Refried beans, heated
Shredded lettuce, tomatoes
  and cheese

Combine pork, tomatoes, cumin, garlic, red pepper, celery, onions and Jalapaneo peppers in a large saucepan. Cook over low heat for 3 hours or until pork is tender. Place ¼ cup heated refried beans on tortilla and roll up. Top with ½ cup sauce, shredded lettuce, tomatoes and cheese. Serves 6.

David Harralson
Oneida County

MØRBRAD MED SVEDSKER OG AEBLER
(Pork Loin Stuffed with Prunes and Apples)
Scandinavian

12 medium prunes, pitted
1 large tart apple, peeled, cored
and cut into 1-inch cubes
1 teaspoon lemon juice
4½-5 pounds boned loin of
pork, center cut
Salt

Freshly ground black pepper
3 tablespoons butter
3 tablespoons vegetable oil
¾ cup dry white wine
¾ cup heavy cream
1 tablespoon red currant jelly

Place prunes in a saucepan, cover with cold water, bring to a boil. Remove from heat and let prunes soak in water for 30 minutes. Drain, pat dry with paper towels, set aside. Sprinkle cubed apples with lemon juice to prevent discoloring. With a strong, sharp knife, make a pocket in the pork by cutting a deep slit down the length of the loin, going to within ½-inch of the two ends and to within 1-inch of the other side. Season the pocket lightly with salt and pepper and stuff it with the prunes and apples, sewing up the opening with strong kitchen thread. Tie the loin at 1-inch intervals to keep its shape while cooking. Preheat oven to 350 degrees. In a casserole equipped with a cover, melt the butter and oil over moderate heat. When the foam subsides, add the loin turning it occasionally with 2 wooden spoons. (Should take about 20 minutes to brown.) Remove all the fat from pan. Pour in wine, stir in heavy cream, whisking briskly and bringing to a simmer on top of stove. Cover and cook in center of oven for 1½ hours, or until meat shows no resistance when pierced with tip of a sharp knife. Remove loin and place on heated platter while you finish sauce. Skim fat from the liquid in the pan and bring the liquid to a boil. When it has reduced to about 1 cup, stir in currant jelly, reduce heat and stirring constantly simmer until smooth. Carve meat in 1-inch slices, pass sauce separately.

Dolores Hansen
Broome County

KALE
German

15 pounds fresh Kale or
6 2-pound cans
2-3 pounds smoked pork
(or smoked butt)
1 large smoked Kielbasa
3-4 medium size grain wurst or
rinkel wurst

2 pounds of small potatoes
1 raw potato, grated
Salt and pepper to taste
1 clove garlic

Note: Special ingredients can be found in a German Delicatessen.

Thoroughly clean Kale—wash each leaf thoroughly 3-4 times if fresh. Place in large pot. Cook Kale down slowly for 2 hours. Add meat ingredients and cook for 1½ hours longer. Cover. Stir occasionally, add more water if needed. Boil 2 pounds of small potatoes in jackets, peel when done. When Kale is completed add raw potato, grated, and mix well. Add other potatoes, sliced and mix. Season to taste. Leftovers can be warmed up in frying pan.

Regina McPhail
Essex County

LAUCHWICKEL
(Leek Rolls)
German

White part of leeks
(2 per person)
Sliced Danish ham
(1 for each leek)
2½ tablespoons butter or
margarine

¼ cup flour
2 cups leek broth
3 ounces tomato paste
½ cup heavy cream
Salt and pepper to taste

Cut off white part of leeks and wash well. Discard green leaves. Boil in salt water until tender (about ½ hour). Fry each slice of ham in some margarine. Wrap one slice of ham around each leek and put into buttered casserole dish. Add the 2½ tablespoons butter or margarine to pan in which ham was fried. Melt and add the flour, stirring until smooth. Very gradually add the broth in which the leeks were boiled, stirring continuously. Add the tomato paste and heavy cream. Season with salt and pepper. Pour this sauce over leeks and bake uncovered in 350 degree oven for ½ hour. May be served with rice, mashed potatoes or potatoes boiled in salt water.

Lore Ufrecht-Ford
Ontario County

GERMAN CABBAGE SUPPER
German

4 tablespoons margarine, divided
4 knockwurst, cut in half lengthwise
1½ pounds cabbage, red and white
1 medium onion, sliced
3 tablespoons white vinegar

⅓ cup brown sugar
1 teaspoon nutmeg
1 teaspoon salt
¼ teaspoon pepper
2 tart apples, cored, peeled, sliced and sprinkled with lemon juice

Melt 2 tablespoons of margarine in a large skillet, add knockwurst and cook until brown on both sides. Remove from skillet. Add remaining margarine, cabbage and onion. Cover and cook about 10 minutes, stirring occasionally. Meanwhile, combine vinegar, brown sugar, nutmeg, salt and pepper. Add to the skillet, cover and bring to a boil. Add apple slices and cook partially covered 10 minutes longer. Add knockwurst and cook just until the meat is heated through. Serves 4-6.

Mrs. Emma Frey
Albany County

SPAGHETTINI CARBONARA
Italian

1 pound bacon
1 medium zucchini
⅓ medium onion
1 pound Italian spaghettini
6 tablespoons butter
1 tablespoon white wine

2 egg yolks
1 pint heavy cream
½ cup Parmesan cheese, grated
Salt
Pepper, freshly ground

Cut bacon in thirds and cook to a crisp in a skillet. Slice onion and zucchini and add to bacon. Cook spaghettini in 4 quarts salted boiling water for 4-5 minutes and drain. Combine butter and wine in large fry pan over medium flame, and let the wine reduce quickly. Place spaghettini in pan and cook for 2 minutes, tossing to coat well with butter and wine. Add egg yolks and cream. Mix quickly so eggs do not scramble. Add bacon and onion and mix well. Add Parmesan cheese, salt and pepper. Mix well. Serve with remaining Parmesan cheese and additional freshly ground pepper. Serves 6.

Steven W. Bancroft
Chautauqua County

BUCATINI ALL 'AMATRICIANA
Italian

2 small white onions, chopped
1 small red pepper, chopped
¼ pound salt pork, diced
3 tablespoons olive oil
8 slices bacon, diced
4 cups (2-pound can) Italian plum tomatoes or 2-pounds fresh tomatoes, peeled and diced

1 pound bucatini (thin macaroni)
2 tablespoons butter
½ cup Romano cheese, grated
Milled black pepper, liberal amount
Salt and pepper to taste

Note: Bucatini refers to type of pasta. Amatriciana refers to the method.

Sauté onions and peppers with the salt pork in the olive oil until pork is nearly crisp, but not too hard, stir, add bacon and cook over low heat for 5 minutes. Blend in tomatoes, mill in pepper, taste for seasoning, stir well and simmer, uncovered, for 40 minutes. Cook bucatini al dente and drain. Place in a large warm bowl with the butter, toss, add the cheese, mill in black pepper and toss again. Serve pasta in individual, hot bowls, with a liberal spooning of the sauce over each portion. Serves 4-6.

Note: A main pasta dish typical to the province of Abruzzi where noted Italian chefs come from.

Mrs. Inez Migliore
Washington County

PORK AND CABBAGE GUYLAS PIE
(SZEKELGULYAS)
With Potato Biscuit
Hungarian

2 tablespoons lard
1¼ pounds boneless lean pork
  shoulder, cut into ¾-inch
  cubes
¾ cup onion, diced
2 teaspoons sweet Hungarian
  paprika
1 clove garlic, crushed
Pinch ground red (cayenne)
  pepper

1 tomato, peeled, seeded,
  chopped
1 pound sauerkraut, drained
  well (if canned is used,
  rinse well)
½ cup dairy sour cream
1 tablespoon all-purpose flour
½ teaspoon caraway seeds
Potato Biscuit

Potato Biscuit:

5 tablespoons riced boiled
  potato
2 tablespoons heavy cream
1 cup all-purpose flour
¾ teaspoon baking powder
¼ teaspoon salt
6 tablespoons unsalted butter,
  cold

3 tablespoons fresh parsley,
  minced
Cold water (optional)
1 egg yolk (lightly beaten with
  1 tablespoon water)

Heat lard in large heavy saucepan or a small Dutch oven over medium-high heat until very hot. Add pork; cook, stirring occasionally, until very brown on all sides (about 12 minutes). Remove pork with slotted spoon and drain on paper toweling. Sauté onion in drippings over medium high heat until lightly browned. Return pork to pan; sprinkle with paprika, garlic, and ground red pepper; stir well. Add tomato and enough water to barely cover ingredients. Heat to boiling, reduce heat. Simmer covered, until pork is tender, about 1½ hours. Add sauerkraut to guylas, simmer 10 minutes. Whisk sour cream, flour and caraway seeds in a small bowl, stir into guylas. Simmer, stirring occasionally, 10 minutes. Meanwhile make potato biscuits. Mix potato and cream in small bowl, refrigerate. Sift flour, baking powder, and salt into medium bowl. Cut in butter until mixture resembles coarse corn meal. Sprinkle parsley over flour mixture, toss to mix. Stir in potato mixture, toss with fork until mixture cleans sides of bowl. (Add cold water 1 teaspoon at a time if needed.) Knead briefly and gently on lightly floured surface. Roll or pat dough to ¼-inch thickness. Cut to fit inside top of 5-cup casserole. Brush biscuit lightly with egg wash. Bake on ungreased

Pork and Cabbage Guylas Pie (continued)

baking sheet 10 minutes, cool slightly on baking sheet on wire rack. Transfer to top of filled casserole and finish baking. Bake at 375 degrees until biscuit is golden brown. Serves 4.

Retha J. Thompson
Clinton County

CHICKEN MARENGO
French

1 2-3 pound frying chicken, cut
   into serving size pieces
⅓ cup flour
1 teaspoon salt
¼ teaspoon pepper
¼ cup olive oil
1 clove garlic, crushed
3 tablespoons onion, chopped
4 tomatoes, quartered
1 cup white wine

1 herb bouquet (4 sprigs
   parsley, 1 sprig thyme, 1 bay
   leaf tied in a cheesecloth bag)
2 tablespoons butter
4 ounces mushrooms, sliced
½ cup green olives, sliced
½ cup cold consommé (½ cup
   hot water and ½ chicken
   bouillon cube)
2 tablespoons flour

Rinse chicken pieces and pat dry. To coat chicken evenly, shake 2 or 3 pieces at a time in a plastic bag containing ⅓ cup flour, 1 teaspoon salt and ¼ teaspoon pepper. Heat ¼ cup of olive oil in a heavy skillet and brown the chicken pieces. Add 1 clove of garlic, crushed, 3 tablespoons chopped onion, 4 tomatoes quartered, 1 cup of white wine and the herb bouquet. Cover and simmer over low heat ½ hour or until thickest pieces of chicken are tender when pierced with a fork. Sauté in small skillet 2 tablespoons of butter and 4 ounces of sliced mushrooms. Add to chicken the ½ cup sliced green olives. Remove the chicken from the skillet and discard the herb bouquet. To thicken the liquid gradually add the ½ cup of cold consommé mixed with 2 tablespoons of flour to mixture in skillet, stirring constantly. Boil 3-5 minutes until mixture thickens. Return chicken to sauce, cover and simmer 10 minutes. Arrange chicken on hot platter. Cover with the sauce. Serves 4-5.

Mrs. Ronald McKotch
Chautauqua County

BITTERBALLEN
(Meatballs)
Dutch

3 tablespoons butter
4 tablespoons flour
1 cup milk or water
1 tablespoon onion, finely chopped
1 teaspoon Worcestershire sauce
½ teaspoon nutmeg

½ teaspoon salt
1½ cups cooked chicken or beef, chopped
Bread crumbs
2 egg yolks
Fat for frying
Mustard

Melt the butter, stir in flour, add milk or water, make a thick sauce. Add the 6 following ingredients. Simmer for 5 minutes, stirring well. Spread mixture on plate and when cool, shape into balls. Roll these in bread crumbs. Beat egg yolks with 3 tablespoons water. Roll balls through this mixture covering well on all sides. Roll again through bread crumbs. Let stand 1 hour. Drop in hot fat (deep fryer) cook until brown, drain on absorbent paper. Serve with mustard.

Note: I make these in large quantities and freeze. They make wonderful hot hors d'oeuvres.

Judith A. Noorlander
Orange County

CHICKEN CUTLETS
Italian

2 pounds breast of chicken, boned, cut into strips
½ cup flour
½ teaspoon salt
2 eggs

2 tablespoons milk
1 tablespoon oil
1 cup Italian bread crumbs
1 cup spaghetti sauce
½ cup Mozzarella cheese

Roll chicken strips in salted flour, then dip into the egg and milk mixture and roll in the bread crumbs. Put the 1 tablespoon of oil in fry pan and heat. Drop cutlets in and fry 2-4 minutes on each side or until brown. Put them in layers in a baking dish. Spoon the spaghetti sauce over each layer and sprinkle with the Mozzarella cheese. Bake at 350 degrees for 15 minutes or until chicken is done.

Francine Brennan
Warren County

ARROZ CON POLLO
(Chicken with Rice)
Spanish-Hispanic

1 2-3 pound chicken cut in
  pieces
4 tablespoons corn oil
2 tablespoons black pepper
½ cup tomato sauce
2 tablespoons olives and
  capers

4 cups water
3 cups rice
Salt to taste
1 can red pimientos

In a casserole heat one tablespoon of oil, fry chicken pieces until brown. Add black pepper, tomato sauce, olives, capers and one cup of water. Cover and simmer for 30 minutes. Add remaining 3 cups of water, bring to boil, add rice and salt to taste. Cook over medium heat until liquid is absorbed. Add remaining oil, cover and cook slowly until rice is cooked about 20 minutes. Stir and cook another 5 minutes. Serve hot and garnish with pimientos. Serves 6.

Eva Colon
Wayne County

POLLO EN CACEROLA
(Chicken Casserole)
Spanish-Hispanic

Note: Prepare on Friday for Sunday

3 cups cooked chicken, cut into
  large pieces
1 can (10 ounce) cream of
  chicken soup, undiluted
⅔ cup sweet peas, drained
1 can marinated chopped
  artichokes

¼ cup sweet red pimientos,
  drained
⅔ cup carrots, diced
¼ cup onions, chopped

Mix all ingredients in 4-quart casserole. Bake in preheated oven, 350 degrees 30-40 minutes. Garnish with slices of hard boiled egg. Serves 6.

Note: Can be prepared and frozen. Thaw completely before baking.

Volunteer
Cayuga County

ORANGE WINE CHICKEN
Jewish

1 large chicken, cut in serving
  pieces
½ stick margarine
1 medium onion, diced
½ cup green pepper, diced
1 tablespoon flour

1 teaspoon salt
¼ teaspoon pepper
1 cup orange juice
¼ cup white wine
1 teaspoon orange peel, grated
1 tablespoon brown sugar

Place chicken in large shallow baking dish. Melt margarine in saucepan. Add onion, pepper and sauté 5 minutes. Blend in flour, salt, pepper, orange juice and wine, stirring until smooth. Stir in brown sugar and orange peel and bring mixture to a boil. Pour over chicken in baking dish at 375 degrees for 45 minutes. Can be served over rice.

Ruth Shapiro
Warren County

LEBANESE CHICKEN AND RICE
Lebanese

1 frying chicken (2½-3 pounds)
1 small onion, cut up
2 celery stalks, cut up
½ pound lamb, diced
1 tablespoon parsley flakes or
  handful fresh parsley
1 tablespoon crushed mint or
  handful fresh mint

½ cup Pignolia nuts,
  "Pine nuts"
Butter
1 cup washed, uncooked rice
3 cups chicken broth
Salt and pepper to taste

Note: Pignolia nuts can be found in any Oriental store.

Cook fryer in water to cover with onion, celery and salt until tender, about 1 hour. Remove chicken and set aside and reserve broth. Sauté diced lamb, add parsley, mint, salt and pepper. In separate pan, brown pine nuts with butter. Mix well with lamb mixture. Add rice and 3 cups chicken broth to mixture. Mix well and cook 30 minutes or until rice is done. Remove chicken from bones, add to the rice, serve hot. Cooking time 1½ hours. Serves 4.

Mrs. George Lewis
Chenango County

CHICKEN VELVET
Oriental

4 Chinese dried mushrooms	1½ teaspoons cornstarch
3 pounds chicken breasts	1 cup snow peas
5 egg whites	Liquid oil
¼ cup water	½ teaspoon salt

Note: The dried mushrooms and snow peas are available at Oriental food stores. Sliced canned mushrooms may be substituted.

Sauce:

½ teaspoon salt	1 tablespoon dry sherry
1 tablespoon cornstarch	
¾ cup rich chicken stock, seasoned	

Soak dried mushrooms in warm water 40 minutes or longer. When soft, remove stems, squeeze out excess water and slice in thin strips. Set aside. Cut off breast meat. Remove skin, pound with smooth mallet between wax paper or plastic wrap until ⅟₁₆-inch thick. Cut into 2-inch wide strips. Pieces can be irregular in size but should be uniform in thickness. Beat egg whites until foamy but not stiff. Gradually add water and cornstarch while beating. Add chicken meat. Wash and trim ends of snow peas. Using a well seasoned skillet, wok or non-stick pan, preheat, then drizzle about one tablespoon of liquid oil in a circle in skillet. Stir-fry fresh green snow peas until bright green and slightly crisp. Remove. Add more oil depending on the type of pan you use. Add chicken and egg mixture. Cook until chicken is white and still tender. Mix all ingredients for sauce and add to skillet. When thickened, add green snow peas and toss. Adjust seasoning to taste. Serves 4-6.

Note: This is a delicate and light dish which can be served with plain or fried rice.

Joyce Nishimura
Chenango County

KHOWPOT SAI GY
(Cow pot sigh guy)
(Fried Rice with Chicken)
Thailand

2 cups rice, wash 3 times in
  cold water and drain
½ chicken or 2 breast halves,
  cooked, cooled and sliced
1 egg
3 tablespoons ketchup

2 tablespoons Nampla
  (fish sauce)
4 tablespoons butter or
  margarine
Salt and pepper to taste
1 onion

Note: Nampla can be found in Fish market or Health Food store.

Cook rice in large saucepan with 4½ cups water about 15 minutes, until not quite cooked. (Bring water and rice to a boil, stir with a fork, then turn heat to low, cover with a tight lid and leave for 15 minutes.) Drain and put back on stove to low fire until dry and fluffy for 10 minutes. Put aside. Put a small amount of butter in a small fry pan and heat. Beat 1 egg well with small amount of water (1 teaspoon), salt and pepper. Pour into fry pan, tip to fill pan, cook 1 minute, turn over to brown. Slide out onto plate, roll up like jelly roll, secure with picks, slice into thin slices.

Cut ½ medium onion into thin slices and cut in ½ again. Cook sliced onions in 1½ tablespoons butter in large skillet until golden. Add chicken slices to onion to cook for 2 minutes, then add 1 teaspoon Nampla, ¼ teaspoon salt, pepper and 2 tablespoons ketchup. Cook slowly 4 minutes. Heat 2 tablespoons butter in large skillet, when hot add the cooked rice. Stir rice constantly to heat, then add 1 tablespoon ketchup and 1 tablespoon Nampla to moisten, with salt and pepper. Add chicken mixture. Stir to mix well over heat, then leave uncovered. Reheat when ready to serve. Put rice, chicken mixture on large platter, garnish with omelette slices. Also make tomato roses for additional color out of patio tomatoes.

Note: Ham, pork or shrimp may be used instead of chicken.

Jean Popp
Delaware County

ORIENTAL CURRIED CHICKEN AND RICE
Oriental

3 tablespoons butter	2 cups cooked rice
3 tablespoons flour	1 cup fresh coconut, shredded
1 teaspoon salt	Peanuts
2 level teaspoons curry powder	Bacon strips
3 cups chicken stock	Hard boiled eggs
3 cups cooked chicken	Grated cheese

Melt butter, add flour, salt and curry powder, add stock and cook 5 minutes. Add chicken. Serve plates with quantity of steamed rice covered with curried chicken. Sprinkle grated coconut over top. Serve side dishes of salted peanuts, bacon strips, hard boiled eggs and grated cheese. Serves 6-8.

Donald O. Benjamin
Royal Savage Inn
Clinton County

INDIAN CHICKEN
Indian

2 pounds of chicken, cut up and skin removed	1 teaspoon paprika
2 medium onions	1 teaspoon cumin powder
2 large cloves of garlic	¼ teaspoon cinnamon
1 large piece of fresh ginger (canned if necessary)	Dash of ground cloves
1 teaspoon turmeric	1½ teaspoons Meat Masala
	1 teaspoon coriander powder
	4 medium tomatoes

Note: You may obtain unusual spices at a Indian Health Food Store.

Wash and remove skin from chicken. Dice onions and fry until light brown in a small amount of oil. Add garlic and finely cut ginger and fry for three minutes. Make a paste of the rest of the powdered spices and add to onion mixture and cook for three more minutes. Add chopped tomatoes and cook until soft. Add chicken pieces, cover and simmer until finished, about 1-1½ hours. I use an electric fry pan.

Note: Serve with NAN, an Indian bread that can be found frozen in Indian Health Food Stores. If bread is not available, serve on hot cooked rice.

Jo-Ann Wadhwa
Dutchess County

SUPREME DE VOLAILLE
French

3 whole chicken breasts	⅓ cup dry white wine
⅓ cup butter	⅓ cup chicken consommé
1 scallion	1 cup heavy cream
¼ pound mushrooms, sliced	Chopped parsley

Sauté cut up breasts after boning in ⅓ cup butter 5 minutes on each side. Remove to a hot platter and keep warm in low oven. Sauté 1 scallion and ¼ pound mushrooms in drippings 5 minutes. Add ⅓ cup wine and ⅓ cup consommé. Cook down until syrupy. Stir in 1 cup cream and cook until slightly thickened. Pour over breast and sprinkle with parsley.

Jean Weiss
Genesee County

SWEET AND SOUR CHICKEN
Oriental

1 chicken fryer	¼ cup chicken stock
Garlic salt	⅓ cup white vinegar
Flour	½ teaspoon salt
2 eggs	1 tablespoon soy sauce
1 cup cooking oil	¼ cup catsup
¾ cup sugar	

Preheat oven to 350 degrees. Cut chicken into small pieces (serving size, halve breast and legs), wipe dry with paper towel, sprinkle with garlic salt and roll in flour. Beat eggs, and dip chicken pieces in eggs until well coated. Put oil in skillet and cook chicken until lightly browned. Drain chicken and place in a shallow casserole dish. Make sauce by mixing sugar, stock, vinegar, salt, soy sauce and catsup; pour over chicken. Bake in 350 degree oven for 1 hour, turning once. Serves 4.

Note: For salt free diets garlic powder may be substituted and salt omitted from sauce.

Teresa L. Bero
Madison County

CHICKEN FAROOQ
Pakistan

2 medium onions, chopped fine
4 cloves of garlic, crushed
½ teaspoon ground red pepper
½ teaspoon salt

1 cup plain yogurt
1 medium chicken, cut up to
   serving size
½ cup vegetable oil

Mix onion, garlic, red pepper and salt with the yogurt. Marinate the chicken in this mixture for 4-5 hours. Heat the oil, remove the chicken from the yogurt mixture and fry in oil until brown on all sides. Drain off all except about 2 tablespoons of the oil. Add the yogurt mixture to the chicken in the pan. Cover and cook on low heat until chicken is tender (about 45 minutes). Serve hot with rice or chapaties (Pakistani flat bread).

Marjorie Abbas
Steuben County

CHICKEN PAPRIKASH
Roumania

8 cups onion, diced
1 whole chicken, cut up
2 tablespoons Hungarian sweet
   paprika
3 tablespoons vegetable oil or
   chicken fat

Salt
1 cup sweet or sour cream
¼ cup parsley, minced

Sauté onions in oil or chicken fat over medium heat for at least 10 minutes, stirring often. Add paprika, stir and cook slowly for at least ten more minutes, until onions are very soft, but never brown.

Add chicken, toss to mix well. Cover pan and cook over medium heat, stirring often to avoid sticking. Simmer for about an hour, or until juice runs clear from chicken thighs, when pierced with a fork. Dish can be made ahead and refrigerated up to this point. Just before serving, mix in sweet or sour cream and parsley, heat through. Serve with rice pilaf and a sharp green salad.

Chazy Dowaliby
Ulster County

CHICKEN PILAF
(PULAO)
Pakistan

2 cups raw Bansati rice (long grain rice can be used)
1 small chicken, cut in 8 pieces
1 small stick cinnamon
1 tablespoon coriander seeds
1 teaspoon cumin seeds
2 cloves garlic
2 small onions, sliced
1 bay leaf
½ teaspoon ginger powder
2 teaspoons salt
½ cup vegetable oil
1 10-inch square clean muslin cloth
4 cups water

Wash and soak rice before using (about ½ hour). In the muslin cloth tie cinnamon, coriander, cumin, cloves of garlic, ½ of onions, bay leaf. In a 4-quart pan put pieces of chicken, water, salt and tied spices, on moderate heat, let it boil until chicken is tender, discard tied spices, separate chicken pieces from broth.

In a 6-quart saucepan put oil and rest of the onions, fry to golden brown. On moderate heat add chicken, ginger and fry for 5 minutes, add chicken broth, let it boil, add rice (soaking water discarded) let it boil until most of the water is absorbed. Turn the heat to low, put the lid on tightly, don't peek for one half hour.

Surraiya Anjum
Schoharie County

COQ AU VIN
French

8 pieces of chicken (4 breasts, halved)
1½ cups Rosé wine
½ cup soy sauce
½ cup oil
1 teaspoon ginger
2 cloves garlic, sliced thin
2 tablespoons brown sugar
½ teaspoon oregano
Few peppercorns

Mix liquids, sugar and spices together and pour over chicken. Bake at 375 degrees for 1 hour, (basting occasionally). Good served with wild rice and a salad.

Barbara Guido
Erie County

QUICK AND EASY PARTY CHICKEN
English

8-10 chicken cutlets (whole
  cutlets that can be split to
  serve 16-20) or (whole breasts
  boned and skinned)
2 cans cream of mushroom
  soup

1 can sliced mushrooms
1½ cups of sour cream
⅓ cup cream sherry wine
Pinch seasoned salt

Split cutlets. Sprinkle with salt. Place in shallow dish. Combine remaining ingredients and pour over chicken. Bake 350 degree oven, 30 minutes covered, then uncover and bake 30 to 45 minutes more. Can be completely prepared in A.M. to be cooked for dinner in P.M.

Marian Durkin
Putnam County

SPANISH PAELLA
Spanish-Hispanic

½ cup flour
2½ teaspoons salt
¼ teaspoon pepper
1 3-pound broiler, sectioned
5 tablespoons margarine
¼ cup water
1 small clove garlic
1 cup raw rice

½ teaspoon saffron
1 chicken bouillon cube
½ cup boiling water
4 cups warm water
1 small onion, sliced
¼ cup green pepper, chopped
1 pound shrimp, cleaned and
  deveined

Combine flour, 1½ teaspoons salt and pepper; coat chicken pieces. Melt 3 tablespoons margarine in a large skillet. Brown chicken. Slowly add ¼ cup water; cover and simmer for 20 minutes.

In a large heavy pot, melt remaining 2 tablespoons margarine with clove of garlic. Add rice, saffron, and remaining 1 teaspoon salt; mix well. Remove garlic. Dissolve bouillon cube in ½ cup boiling water. Combine chicken broth and warm water; slowly pour into rice mixture. Add chicken, onion and green pepper. Cook uncovered for 20 minutes. Add shrimp and cook an additional 5 minutes or until shrimp is done.

Place mixture in a 3-quart casserole. Heat in a moderate oven 325 degrees for 15 minutes. Serves 6.

Margaret C. Capacci
Seneca County

CHINESE COOKING WITH LEFTOVERS
Oriental

2 cups chicken or turkey, (leftover)
1 cup celery, diced
1 cup green peppers, diced
¼ cup onions, diced
(can include 1 cup of other fresh vegetables, i.e., cauliflower, broccoli, mushrooms, asparagus, etc.)

¼ cup vegetable oil
1 teaspoon chicken bouillon
½ cup water
2 teaspoons cornstarch
3 tablespoons cooking wine
6 tablespoons soy sauce
1 cup cooked rice

Assuming meat is already cooked from a previous meal, heat vegetable oil in skillet then stir-fry vegetables until tender (but slightly crisp). Add meat and stir for few minutes to combine flavor of meat and vegetables. In bowl mix remaining ingredients—adding cornstarch last. Add mixture to meat and vegetables, stirring slowly until liquid thickens. Add water until consistency is to your liking. Serve over rice. Can substitute with beef bouillon.

Karin Franklin
Onondaga County

TURKEY CHOW MEIN
Oriental

3 cups turkey, diced
2 cups onion, quartered and sliced
3 tablespoons salad oil
2 cups celery, sliced in spears
½ teaspoon salt

⅛ teaspoon pepper
1½ cups turkey stock or water
2 #2 cans oriental vegetables, drained (1 sprouts, 1 mixed vegetables)

Sauce:
⅔ cup cold water
4 tablespoons cornstarch

4 teaspoons soy sauce
2 teaspoons sugar

Add meat and onion to oil, sauté until onion is golden, stirring often. Add celery, salt, pepper, water, cooking 5 minutes. Add drained vegetables and heat to simmering. Blend sauce mixture, add and simmer 5 minutes. Serve on rice, or chow mein noodles, crisped in the oven, with rice as a side dish. Serves 8-10.

Ruth Cicchinelli
Tioga County

TURKEY ENCHILADAS
Mexican

Oil
2 4-ounce cans green chilies
1 large clove garlic, minced
1 (1-pound, 12-ounce can)
  tomatoes, drained
2 cups onions, chopped
2 teaspoons salt

½ teaspoon oregano
½ cup water or tomato liquid
3 cups cooked turkey, shredded
2 cups sour cream, (non-dairy
  substitute)
2 cups Cheddar cheese, grated
1 package corn tortillas (15)

Heat 2 tablespoons oil to 300 degrees in electric skillet. Rinse seeds from chilies and chop (use rubber gloves and don't touch eyes). Sauté garlic and chilies. Add tomatoes (broken up), onion, 1 teaspoon salt, oregano and ½ cup water. Simmer at 200 degrees uncovered for 30 minutes. Remove from pan and put aside.

Combine turkey, sour cream, grated cheese, and remaining salt. Heat ⅓ cup oil and dip tortillas until they are limp. Drain on paper towel. Fill with turkey mixture, roll up and place seam side down in skillet. Pour chili sauce over and cook at 250 degrees for 20 minutes or until warmed through.

Note: This is a good way to use leftover turkey or chicken. If you prefer less spicy foods, you can decrease the chilies or eliminate them and use more tomatoes in the sauce.

Mary Anne Perks
Chemung County

SHRIMP RÉMOULADE
French

6 tablespoons olive oil
2 tablespoons vinegar
1 tablespoon paprika
½ teaspoon pepper
4 teaspoons mustard with
  horseradish

1 celery heart, chopped fine
½ white onion, chopped
½ teaspoon parsley, chopped
½ teaspoon salt
1 pound shrimp

Mix first five ingredients together well, then add remainder and mix again. Test for seasoning and add more salt if necessary. Cover and chill in refrigerator until ready to serve. Serve over prepared cooked, chilled shrimp about 1 pound on a bed of shredded lettuce leaves. Serves 2.

Note: Rémoulade is a cold sauce that can also be used on cold cut up chicken or beef.

Volunteer
Allegany County

SHRIMP SCAMPI FOR TWO
Italian

4 eggs
12 shrimp, cooked, shelled
   and deveined
1 cup flour
⅔ cup olive oil

¼ stick butter, melted
¼ cup Marsala wine
8-10 mushroom caps, fresh
Garlic salt
Rosemary

Beat eggs in bowl, pad shrimp with flour and dip each one into eggwash. Preheat 10-inch pan with oil over medium heat. Fry shrimp until golden brown. Drain oil. Add butter, mushrooms, Marsala wine and garlic salt, rosemary to taste. Simmer 2-3 minutes. Serve.

Note: Complemented by a fine steak or Fettucine Alfredo.

Volunteer
Broome County

TUNA ST. JACQUES
French

3 green onions, chopped fine
4 tablespoons butter or
   margarine
4-ounce can sliced mushrooms,
   drained
1 can (10½-ounce) cream of
   chicken soup
½ cup dry vermouth
White pepper to taste

1 tablespoon parsley, chopped
   fine (fresh is best)
2 cans (7-ounces each) white
   meat tuna, drained and
   chunked
2 tablespoons Parmesan
   cheese
1 slice bread, crust removed

Preheat oven to 450 degrees. Cook onions in 2 tablespoons butter until tender. Add 1 tablespoon additional butter and mushrooms. Sauté 1 minute. Combine soup and vermouth. Heat to boiling. Season to taste. Add onions, mushrooms, tuna and parsley. Spoon equally into 6 buttered sea shells. Combine bread and cheese in blender. Sprinkle over sauce. Drizzle 1 tablespoon melted butter over crumbs. Heat in oven 10 minutes or until browned. Serves 6.

Note: 8-ounce cooked small can of shrimp can be substituted for 1 can of tuna. Shells can be prepared early in day and baked at last minute. An easy, inexpensive but elegant company dish.

Dorothea Allen Fowler
Cortland County

SALMON PUFF
English

3 tablespoons margarine
3 tablespoons flour
Salt to season
½ teaspoon mustard
½ teaspoon Worcestershire
  sauce

1 cup milk
4 eggs, separated
16-ounce can salmon

One hour and 15 minutes before dinner; grease 1½-quart baking dish. In saucepan melt margarine. Stir in flour, salt, mustard and Worcestershire sauce until blended. Slowly stir in milk. Cook until thick, stirring constantly. Cool 10 minutes. Beat in egg yolks, one at a time. In a bowl, break up salmon, do not drain. Stir into mixture. In a large bowl, beat egg whites until stiff. Fold into mixture and pour into baking dish. Bake in 375 degree oven for 40-45 minutes. Serve immediately.

Mary Suffredini
Seneca County

CIOPPINO
Italian

1 medium onion, chopped
1 large green pepper, chopped
6 cloves garlic, minced
3 tablespoons vegetable oil
3 tablespoons butter
1 tablespoon parsley
2 teaspoons oregano
1 cup sherry

1 cup white wine
1 pound fish filets (red snapper,
  perch or sole)
1 pound bay scallops
1 pound king crab legs
2 dozen large shrimp, cleaned
2 dozen clams, scrubbed
1 pound linguini, cooked

In a large pot, sauté onion, pepper and garlic in oil and butter until cooked but not browned (about 15 minutes). Add parsley, oregano, sherry and wine. Let simmer about one hour. Add fish, scallops, crab legs, shrimp and clams. Cook about 20 minutes or until all clams are opened. To serve, spread linguini on a large platter and top with the fish mixture. Serve with a large basket of garlic bread on the side.

Mrs. Arnold Kip
Dutchess County

FISH SOUFFLÉ
(Fiskegratin)
Norwegian

½ cup butter
⅔ cup flour
2 cups milk
¼ teaspoon salt
Dash of pepper
⅛ teaspoon nutmeg

4 egg yolks
4 egg whites
1½ cups cooked fish, flaked
Bread crumbs
Butter

Prepare a good thick white sauce of the butter, flour, and milk. Add salt and pepper. Add finely flaked fish to the sauce together with grated nutmeg. Cool. Stir in the egg yolks, slightly beaten and fold in the stiffly beaten egg whites. Pour into a buttered baking dish, cover with a good layer of grated bread crumbs made from oven-dried bread, dot with butter and bake in hot oven for 45 minutes. Serve with melted butter. If spice is not used in the soufflé, finely chopped parsley may be added to the butter. Serves 6.

Ellen Strivings
Wyoming County

LUAU FISH WITH COCONUT CREAM
Hawaiian

1 package frozen chopped
   spinach (thaw before
   cooking)
2 teaspoons seasoned salt
2 tablespoons flour
1½-2 pounds fish fillet

½ teaspoon lemon juice
1 cup coconut milk (not
   coconut cream)
½ cup skimmed milk
½ cup coconut
¼ cup bread crumbs

In casserole dish, place spinach on bottom. Combine 1 teaspoon salt and flour and sprinkle on spinach. Place fish on top and sprinkle with lemon juice, flour and salt mixture. Combine coconut milk, skim milk and pour over fish. Bake in 350 degree oven for 35-45 minutes. Combine coconut, bread crumbs and 1 teaspoon seasoned salt and sprinkle on top of fish 15 minutes before fish is done.

Rose Ajimine
Warren County

VEAL FRANCAISE
French

1 pound veal cutlets
1 cup flour
4 eggs
1 teaspoon parsley
1 teaspoon grated cheese
½ teaspoon basil
½ teaspoon garlic powder

Dash of salt and pepper
½ cup oil
½ cup sherry wine
1 cup chicken bouillon or broth
¼ stick butter or margarine
2 lemons

Pound veal cutlets. Roll in flour. Mix eggs, parsley, cheese, basil, garlic powder, salt and pepper together in flat bowl. Dip floured veal in egg mixture and fry in hot oil in skillet. Brown well over medium heat then turn and brown other side. In separate skillet heat sherry, bouillon, and butter to boiling. Place browned veal in sherry mixture. Squeeze juice of two lemons over top of veal. Simmer about 10 minutes. (Can be kept simmering or in oven on a low setting for up to 1 hour).

Note: This recipe is very good with sautéed onions, green peppers, mushrooms and artichoke hearts simmered in a sherry and served over top. Also can be used with filet of sole or boneless chicken breast instead of veal.

Jean Gauthier
Cayuga County

VEAL CACCIATORE
(Italian Veal Stew)
Italian

3 tablespoons olive oil
2 garlic cloves, minced
2 pounds veal stew meat, cut in
  1-inch cubes
3 tablespoons dried oregano
4 ounces dry red wine
1 medium green pepper, cut in
  thin strips

¼ teaspoon black pepper
2 1-pound cans whole peeled
  tomatoes
1 4-ounce can sliced
  mushrooms

In heavy frying pan, over medium high heat, sauté garlic. Add veal and oregano. Brown meat on all sides. Turn heat to low setting and add wine. Simmer uncovered for 3 minutes. Add black pepper and canned tomatoes, cutting tomatoes into small pieces. Stir in mushrooms and green pepper. Cook, uncovered, at low boil for one hour, stirring occasionally.

Mrs. Robert E. Campo
Herkimer County

ZURICH SHREDDED VEAL
Swiss

1 pound veal, lean, cut into fine slivers
1 tablespoon flour
½ cup butter, clarified
1 tablespoon onion, finely diced
1 cup mushrooms, cut into thick slices
½ cup dry white wine
1 cup brown sauce, fairly thick (canned beef gravy may be used)
½ cup fresh cream
½ teaspoon salt
¼ teaspoon black pepper, crushed

Sprinkle veal with flour, sauté in butter quickly over high heat in 10-inch pan (do not overcook veal). Remove from skillet and keep warm, preferably on a sieve to release excess butter from sautéing. Remove excess butter from pan. Add onion and mushrooms and sauté quickly for one minute. Add the wine, reduce by half its volume. Pour in brown sauce, simmer until a heavy consistency has been achieved. Finish the sauce by mixing in the cream, salt, and pepper, bring to a boil. Add the veal slivers and immediately remove from the heat to avoid toughening the meat. (The sauce should be creamy and not too thin.) Serve with Swiss style hashed browned potatoes or spatzle or noodles.

Note: Clarified butter is made by melting butter over low heat and using only the resulting clear liquid, discarding the milky residue.

Mrs. Emma M. Ladd
Wyoming County

VEAL CUTLET SCALOPPINI
Italian

1 slice veal cutlet, cut in strips
3 green peppers, cut in strips
1 whole clove garlic
1 small onion, sliced thin in
 circles
¼ teaspoon hot pepper seeds
2 tablespoons fresh or frozen
 parsley, chopped

1 teaspoon salt
1 quart (home canned) or 1
 #2½ can tomatoes, crushed
1 6-ounce can tomato paste
1 6-ounce can sliced
 mushrooms
1 #1 size can peas

Sauté first 7 ingredients until tender but not too brown, about 15 or 20 minutes. Add tomatoes and paste, bring to boil. Turn heat down and simmer 1 hour, until thick. Do not cover—steam will tend to make it watery. Add drained peas and mushrooms, heat and serve.

Note: Delicious served on rice or noodles with tossed salad and garlic bread.

Mrs. Joseph DeDominick
Schuyler County

SPALTZI
German

2 cups lentils
3 cups water

1½ teaspoons vinegar
1 teaspoon salt

Check lentils for small stones. Wash in 2-quart pot, let sit overnight. (You may want to add 1 cup ham or cut up franks, or add a ham bone while you cook lentils). Cook for 1½ hours on low heat.

Spaltzi:
2 cups flour
2 eggs

¾ cup of water

In medium bowl mix flour, water and eggs. The dough should not be too loose. On a cutting board, put part of dough, cut into pieces as small as possible. Place into 1-quart pot of boiling water. When the pieces of spaltzi float, they are done.

Note: Serve spaltzi on a platter. Serve lentils in separate dish. If you don't add meat add a stick of butter to the lentils when serving.

Berta Killenberger
Schoharie County

CHEESE AND POTATO PIEROGI
Polish

Filling:

1 small onion
½ stick butter or margarine
1 pound pressed cheese,
  broken into small pieces or
  1 pound cottage cheese

1 egg, slightly beaten
Pepper to taste
2 or 3 medium-sized potatoes,
  cooked and mashed

Dough:

2 cups all-purpose flour
1 teaspoon salt

1 egg, slightly beaten
½ cup water (approximately)

Sauté onion in butter and add to mashed potatoes. Blend in the pressed cheese, egg and pepper. Mix together well and set aside. In a large bowl, sift flour and salt together. Add beaten egg and mix well. Add water a little at a time, working dough well. Knead on lightly floured pastry board (about 5 minutes) until firm. Roll out thin and cut circles with cutter or glass. Place a small spoonful of cheese filling on each round of dough. Fold over pressing edges together. Moisten edges with water if necessary to make sure they are well sealed. In a large kettle, bring water to a boil and carefully drop pierogi into the water leaving kettle uncovered. Bring the pierogi to a boil (about 5-8 minutes). Lower heat slightly when they begin to boil. Spoon out pierogi into colander and drain. Pour melted butter over pierogi. You can also heat them in a frying pan. Yield: 24.

Mrs. Stan Tonko
Montgomery County

CABBAGE DUNKING BOWL
Polish

1 small cabbage head
1 cup mayonnaise
1 tablespoon onion, minced
1 tablespoon Bread-and-Butter
  Pickles, finely chopped

1 tablespoon anchovy paste
¼ teaspoon salt
¼ teaspoon pepper

Clean and wash cabbage head. Hollow out center of cabbage for dip. (Save for cole-slaw). Refrigerate until ready to serve. Put remaining ingredients into blender; blend. Fill hollowed-out cabbage head with dip just before serving. Makes 1 cup.

Volunteer
Genesee County

SPANAKOPITTA
(Spinach Pie)
Greek

2-3 pounds young spinach
½ pound onions
1½ cups olive oil
½ cup parsley, chopped
½ cup dill, chopped
1 bunch scallions, chopped

8-10 thin pastry sheets (Phyllo)
    or roll out a double pie crust,
    large size
1½ pounds feta cheese
Salt and pepper to taste

Clean spinach, if the stems are coarse, separate them from the leaves. Wash the spinach well in plenty of water and cut it fine, as for a salad. Combine the spinach, parsley, dill and scallions in a large bowl, salt and set aside for 10 minutes. Drain and squeeze out water. Chop onions and brown in oil. Add to the other vegetables, add cheese and mix well. Season with salt and pepper. Grease a shallow baking pan and line with 4-5 pastry sheets, one on top of the other. Brush each sheet with oil to prevent them from sticking to each other. If pie crust is used, use half the dough for the undercrust and the other half for the overcrust. Put the filling over the bottom crust, spreading evenly, then cover with the rest of the pastry sheets. Brush the top with oil, and with the point of a sharp knife, trace the crust into square pieces. Bake 350 degrees for about 40 minutes. When golden brown, remove from oven, cool and cut.

The Spot Restaurant
Broome County

COLD MARINATED EGGPLANT
Pakistan

1 small eggplant
½ cup celery, chopped
⅓ cup pimiento
1 small clove garlic, minced
2 tablespoons parsley, chopped

¼ teaspoon oregano
½ teaspoon salt
⅛ teaspoon pepper
⅓ cup salad oil
⅓ cup vinegar

Cook eggplant in boiling salted water about 20 minutes or until just tender. Drain, cool, peel and cut in 2-inch lengths. Yield: 2 cups. Add remaining ingredients to the eggplant and mix well. Cover tightly and store in refrigerator. Serve cold. Serves 6.

Volunteer
Lewis County

EGGPLANT PARMIGIANA
Italian

2 eggplants
½ cup flour
1 or 2 eggs (as needed), slightly beaten
½ teaspoon salt
½ teaspoon pepper

1 cup olive oil
2 ounces Parmesan or Romano cheese, grated
1 pound Mozzarella cheese, sliced thin

Tomato sauce:
1 small onion, chopped
2 cloves garlic
4 tablespoons olive oil
1 16-ounce can plum tomatoes, Italian style
½ can tomato paste (dissolved in water)

1 cup water
1 teaspoon sugar (optional)
1 teaspoon basil leaf, chopped
Salt and pepper to taste

Preheat oven to 400 degrees. Pare eggplant and cut into very thin slices. Sprinkle each slice with salt and pile slices on a plate and cover with a weight to draw out juice. Let stand in this manner for about one hour. Next flour eggplant slices and dip into beaten egg seasoned with salt and pepper. Fry in olive oil until slices are golden brown on both sides. Drain on paper towel. Place layer of fried eggplant in casserole, cover with sauce, sprinkle with grated cheese and cover with a layer of Mozzarella. Repeat layers. Bake in hot oven for 15 minutes and serve hot. Serves 4-6.

Mrs. Mary DelVecchio
Greene County

SPINACH ROLL
Italian

Dough:

4 cups flour
¾ teaspoon salt
2 eggs, slightly beaten

2 tablespoons vegetable
   shortening
¾-1 cup boiling water

Filling:

3 10-ounce boxes frozen
   spinach
15 ounces Ricotta cheese
1½ cups Parmesan cheese,
   grated
¼ cup butter, melted

¾ teaspoon salt
¼ teaspoon pepper
Whole nutmeg, few gratings
4 cups tomato sauce
Parmesan cheese

Dough—Add flour and salt in large bowl, make well in center, place eggs and shortening in well, measure water, mix gradually into flour to make a stiff dough. Turn dough onto lightly floured board, knead 5 minutes (until smooth and shiny). Cover and allow to cool 10 minutes.

Filling—Drain thawed spinach, add Ricotta, Parmesan, melted butter, salt, pepper and nutmeg. Mix. Divide dough into 3 parts. Roll to 22-inches x 10-inches on floured board. Spread ⅓ filling on dough. Roll like jelly roll. Place seam down in center of cheesecloth. Roll and tie ends. Heat salt water to boiling. Place one roll at a time in water. Boil 20 minutes, or until roll floats on top. Cool. (Can be frozen at this point).
Remove cheesecloth, cut into 30 slices. Place in 13-inch x 9-inch pan. Cover with tomato sauce. Top with Parmesan cheese. Bake 35 minutes at 350 degrees.

Note: Instead of tomato sauce, olive oil and garlic, or a white sauce with cheese on top can be used. These can also be served as Hors d'oeuvres.

Dorothea Spinelli
Saratoga County

ZUCCHINI QUICHE
(Crustless)
Italian

2 cups zucchini, coarsely
  shredded
¼ cup onion, chopped
4 eggs, beaten
1½ cups skim milk
1 tablespoon all-purpose flour
⅛ teaspoon ground nutmeg
⅛ teaspoon pepper
¼ teaspoon salt

1½ cups Monterey Jack cheese
  (6 ounces), shredded
1 4-ounce can sliced
  mushrooms, drained
1 teaspoon cornstarch
¼ teaspoon dried oregano,
  crushed
1 8-ounce can stewed tomatoes,
  finely cut up

In a covered saucepan, cook zucchini and onion in a small amount of boiling salted water for 5 minutes. Drain well. Press out excess liquid. In a bowl combine eggs, milk, flour, salt, pepper and nutmeg. Stir in cheese, mushrooms and zucchini mixture. Pour into greased 10 x 6 x 2-inch baking dish. On oven rack place, baking dish in a larger pan to a depth of 1-inch of water. Bake 325 degrees for one hour or until knife inserted off center comes out clean. Let stand 10 minutes. Meanwhile combine cornstrch, oregano, dash of salt in a small sauce pan. Stir in tomatoes. Cook until mixture thickens and bubbles. Cook 1 or 2 minutes. Spoon sauce over zucchini lightly. Pass remaining sauce. Serves 5.

Kitty Peterson
Seneca County

LUKSCHEN (NOODLE) KUGEL
Jewish

3 cups broad noodles
4 eggs, beaten
½-¾ cup chicken fat, oil, or
  margarine

Salt to taste
1½ cups raisins
Cinnamon and sugar to taste,
  (optional)

Cook noodles in boiling (salted) water for 10 minutes. Drain and add other ingredients. Place in a well greased baking dish and bake at 400 degrees until top is well browned, about 30 minutes.

Volunteer
Rensselaer County

GERMAN SAUERBRATEN
German

2 cups wine vinegar
2 cups water
¼ cup packed brown sugar
1 tablespoon salt
½ teaspoon pepper
½ teaspoon ground cloves
2 bay leaves

3 medium onions, chopped
2 large carrots, diced
1½ cups celery, diced
2 tablespoons oil or bacon
  drippings
1 teaspoon ground ginger
3-4 pound venison roast

In a large bowl, combine all ingredients. Cover with foil paper and place in refrigerator. Marinate for 3 full days. Turn meat two to three times a day. Be sure never to pierce meat with a fork. On the fourth day, remove meat from juices and vegetables, setting mixture aside to use later. Place meat in Dutch oven, over medium heat and brown well on all sides. Pour in juice and vegetables, simmer covered 2½ to 3 hours or until meat is tender. Serve with potato dumplings.

Gloria Taylor
Sullivan County

PIEROGIS
Polish

Dough:
6 cups flour
¼ pound butter, melted
½ cup milk

3 whole eggs
½ pint sour cream
1 teaspoon salt

Cheese Filling:
1 pound farmer cheese or
  cottage cheese

1 tablespoon sugar
2 eggs

Combine flour and salt. Add butter, milk, eggs and sour cream. Mix to a soft dough. Knead on board a few minutes. Divide in half and roll thin. Cut circles with a large biscuit cutter. Place small spoonful filling a little to one side of each round dough. Moisten edges with water. Fold over and press firmly making sure edges are well sealed. Drop pierogi into salted, boiling water. Cook gently for 3-5 minutes.

Helen B. Morien
Orleans County

GREEK CHEESE OMELET
Greek

1 tablespoon butter
¼ cup finely diced green
  pepper
4 eggs

2 teaspoons milk
½ cup crumbled feta cheese
Pepper to taste

Melt butter in large frying pan. Add green pepper and sauté until tender. Remove from heat. Lift peppers from pan with slotted spoon to allow butter to remain. Beat eggs and milk until frothy. Mix in cheese, pepper to taste and sautéed peppers. Return frying pan to a low heat. When butter is hot, pour in eggs. Turn when set around edges. Cook second side until done. Fold omelet and serve. 4 servings.

Volunteer
St. Lawrence County

BAKED MACARONI ITALIAN STYLE
Italian

1½ pounds Ricotta cheese
6 eggs
1 tablespoon parsley flakes
½ cup Italian cheese, grated

⅛ teaspoon salt
¼ cup milk
1 pound ziti macaroni

Boil ziti macaroni in six-quart saucepan until done, strain. In large bowl, mix together first 5 ingredients, then add cooked ziti. Pour into a baking pan. Pour ¼ cup milk over top and dot with butter. Bake at 350 degrees until golden, about 1 hour.

Doris Lampariello
Delaware County

CHEESE BLINTZE SOUFFLE
Jewish

¼ pound butter (1 stick), melted
18 frozen cheese blintzes
1 pint sour cream

6 eggs
½ cup sugar
1 teaspoon vanilla

Preheat oven to 350 degrees. Melt butter and pour into 9-inch x 13-inch pan (glass or aluminum). Spread evenly. Place all frozen blintzes in pan in rows. Using blender or electric beater beat together the pint of sour cream, eggs, sugar and vanilla. Pour over blintzes. Bake in oven for one hour at 350 degrees. Serve while hot. Optional dressing or plain sour cream makes an added touch of flavor. Serves 8-10.

Note: Optional dressing or sauce: Mix additional sour cream with Jam or Canned fruit. Makes an excellent entrée for Sunday Brunch.

Janet Magill
Monroe County

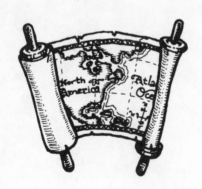

Salads and Salad Dressings

SYBIL LUDINGTON

Sybil Ludington, of English descent, was only 16 years of age when she made Revolutionary War history.

Colonel Ludington, her father, was in command of a volunteer regiment which lived in the countryside surrounding the hamlet of Fredericksburg, New York, which is now known as Ludingtonville.

On April 26, 1777, a messenger reached Colonel Henry Ludington's house at about nine o'clock, to tell him that the English forces were burning Danbury, and that the troops had to be called together. Since the messenger (and his horse) were too exhausted to reach anyone else, and her father was busy organizing, Sybil volunteered to go out and warn the countryside.

In a matter of minutes she was in the saddle and galloped off into the night with only a stick in her hand with which to hit the horse and knock on the doors. It has been said that in comparison with Paul Revere's ride, Sybil's ride was much more difficult. She covered 40 miles of narrow, unmarked, ox-cart roads in order to warn the families and to muster the troops.

Due to Sybil Ludington's efforts more than 400 motley clothed but determined officers and men assembled and marched 25 miles to join General Wooster's forces at Ridgefield and from there helped to drive the Redcoats back to their ships on Long Island Sound.

WINTER SALAD
English

2 medium-sized regular
 cabbage
4 sweet red peppers
4 sweet green peppers
2 large carrots
8 medium onions

4 cups vinegar (white)
3 cups sugar
1 tablespoon salt
1 tablespoon celery seed
1 tablespoon mustard seed
1 teaspoon turmeric

Choose a large work area, then shred cabbage into a large pile. Also create piles of red and green peppers sliced wafer thin, chopped carrots, and wafer thin sliced onions which will separate into rings. Select a large crock or two—one gallon plastic or mayonnaise jars and drop the various ingredients into the container by handfuls to mix. In a large pan, mix the vinegar, sugar, salt, celery seed, mustard seed, and turmeric; heat to the boiling point, and immediately pour over the ingredients in the crock or jars. Be sure that all of the cabbage mixture is completely submerged, if necessary, mix more brine, placing a cover over the containers to allow them to steam and wilt the cabbage. There is no necessity for a tight seal as the containers are to be placed in a cool area such as a basement and allowed to stand for 3-4 weeks before tasting. Once a week it is good to check to be sure that everything is covered with brine and to give the contents a good stir with a spoon. This salad is inexpensive to make when all of the produce is available on the farmer's market in the late fall, and can be enjoyed all winter as it will keep well if kept cool, but, not allowed to freeze. When unexpected company arrives, it can be served with any meat and is also very good with fried fish.

Note: Be sure to pack the jars firmly!

Ronald W. Coombe
Onondaga County

RAW SPINACH SALAD
Greek

1 pound fresh spinach
½ cup diced feta cheese
¼ cup olive oil

Juice of 1 lemon
½ teaspoon salt
Pepper to taste

Wash spinach several times, drain thoroughly. Place in bowl and sprinkle with feta cheese. Combine remaining ingredients. Beat until creamy. Drizzle over spinach. Toss to mix. Serve immediately.

Volunteer
Putnam County

GREEN SALAD
French Dressing
French

½ teaspoon salt
1 clove garlic
½ teaspoon mustard
1 tablespoon vinegar
3 tablespoons salad oil

Worcestershire sauce
¼ head of lettuce
Salt and pepper
Chopped parsley
2 tomato wedges

Put ¼ teaspoon salt in a wooden salad bowl, crush a clove of garlic with a fork and rub the bowl to give a garlic flavor. Remove the garlic pieces. Mix the mustard, vinegar, salad oil and a touch of Worcestershire sauce. Break the lettuce with a wooden fork and spoon, add salt and pepper and mix well.

Volunteer
Hamilton County

DUTCH LETTUCE
Dutch

1 head of lettuce
½ cup salad dressing
2 tablespoons sugar
¼ teaspoon salt
1 tablespoon vinegar

1 tablespoon water (if you
   like it milder)
1 small onion, chopped
1 hard-boiled egg

Wash, drain and tear lettuce in pieces; place in large bowl; set aside. Blend salad dressing, sugar, salt, vinegar, water, pour over lettuce. Add onion and sliced hard-boiled egg, toss together.

Harriet Hyman
Wayne County

ITALIAN ANTIPASTOS
Italian

Arrange on a serving platter:
Sliced hard-boiled egg
Tuna fish
Sliced ham
2 sardines

Sautéed mushrooms with oil
   and vinegar
Lettuce

Sprinkle with oil if desired. Serves 1.

Volunteer
Livingston County

TABOULEY
Lebanese

¾ cup cracked wheat
Salt, pepper and Allspice to taste
2 teaspoons dried peppermint, crushed
2 bunches parsley, washed, chopped finely

3 medium tomatoes
1 bunch green onions
½ cup oil
Juice of lemon

Rinse cracked wheat and drain. Add salt, pepper, allspice and mint leaves, mix thoroughly. Add chopped parsley, tomatoes, onions, mix well. Pour oil over mixture and squeeze lemon over it. Mix thoroughly.

Marie Zogby
Oneida County

GERMAN POTATO SALAD
German

4 pounds new potatoes
½ onion, grated
4 tablespoons sugar
4 tablespoons white vinegar
4 tablespoons water

Dry mustard, pinch
White pepper, pinch
1 scant tablespoon salt
1-2 cups mayonnaise

Boil potatoes in skin (approximately 25-35 minutes) until they can be pricked with a fork. Drain water and leave covered in pot. Peel potatoes while hot with rubber gloves. Cool in refrigerator (2 hours). Slice thinly. Heat onion, sugar, vinegar, water, mustard, salt and pepper until sugar is dissolved. Pour dressing in serving bowl. Add potatoes. Mix with hands (to avoid breaking potatoes). Let sit overnight. Drain dressing. Add mayonnaise just before serving.

Jeanne Agnew
Saratoga County

WARSAW SALAD
Polish

2 medium-size cucumbers
6 large white radishes
2 Delicious apples
½ cup sour cream
2 tablespoons lemon juice

1 tablespoon fresh parsley,
  finely chopped
1 teaspoon black pepper,
  freshly ground

Wash cucumbers and radishes thoroughly; slice them paper-thin. Combine. Wash and core apples; slice into thin slices. Add to vegetables; toss to mix. Combine sour cream and lemon juice. To serve, place vegetable and fruit mixture in serving bowl, top with dressing. Garnish salad with chopped parsley and freshly ground black pepper. Serves 4.

Volunteer
Herkimer County

PRUNES AND BARLEY
Polish

1 1-pound box of prunes
1½ cups of water
1¼-inch slice of fresh lemon
  (optional)
1 cup raisins
1 cup barley

3 cups water
3 tablespoons sugar
1 tablespoon butter or
  margarine
⅛ teaspoon salt

In a medium sized saucepan, cook one pound of prunes in 1½ cups of water with one ¼-inch thick slice of fresh lemon for 15 minutes. Allow mixture to cool enough to handle, and remove pits from prunes, reserving liquid. Remove the lemon slice and discard. Return pitted prunes to the liquid, add one cup of raisins and bring mixture to a boil. Remove from heat, cover and let stand. In a large saucepan, cook one cup of barley in three cups of water until barley has absorbed all the water (approximately 20 minutes). To the hot barley, add sugar, butter or margarine, salt and prune-raisin mixture. Mix well but carefully not mashing the barley. Cover and let stand 5 minutes. This side dish is now ready to be served or can be refrigerated. It may be served hot or cold and is an excellent accent to a ham dinner.

Mrs. Harry Maio
Steuben County

TABOULEH
(Cracked Wheat Salad)
Armenian

1 cup medium cracked wheat
3 cups fresh parsley, finely
  chopped
1 cup fresh mint, finely
  chopped (if available)
1½ cups green onion, finely
  chopped, including green
  tops

4 large ripe tomatoes, cubed
1 cucumber, finely cubed
½ cup vegetable oil
½ cup lemon juice
1 tablespoon tomato paste
Salt and pepper to taste

Place cracked wheat in a large bowl, cover with cold water and let stand for 3 minutes. Drain off water and let stand for 10 minutes. Add vegetables and seasoning, mix well. Add oil, lemon juice and tomato paste. Mix thoroughly.

Peg Kutchukian
Chemung County

FRENCH CARROT SALAD
French

1-pound fresh carrots, scraped
⅓ cup fresh parsley, chopped
¼ cup green onion (scallions),
  finely chopped
⅓ cup fresh parsley, finely
  chopped

½ teaspoon garlic, minced
3 tablespoons olive oil
  (or salad oil)
2 tablespoons vinegar
1 tablespoon lemon juice
1 tablespoon sugar

Finely shred carrots, the pound will yield about 4-5 cups shredded carrots. Add parsley, onion, and garlic. Add remaining ingredients, toss all, and adjust with additional oil or vinegar according to taste. Let stand 1 hour to blend flavors. Sprinkle second ⅓ cup fresh parsley over top as garnish. An inexpensive and vitamin filled salad. Serves 6-8.

Georgette Casavant
Ulster County

ZITI SALAD
Italian

4 medium tomatoes, sliced thin
1 green pepper, sliced thin
½ cup olive oil
1 teaspoon salt
Pepper to taste
1 teaspoon basil

½ teaspoon oregano
1 pound ziti
1 8-ounce package Mozzarella
  cheese, cubed
1 can black olives (optional)
Parmesan cheese

Cook ziti. Combine tomatoes, pepper, oil, salt, pepper, basil, oregano in a large bowl, add cooked ziti (hot and well drained). Add remaining ingredients and stir thoroughly. Sprinkle Parmesan over top, serve immediately.

Lorraine Trombly
Essex County

BEAN SPROUT AND WATER CHESTNUT SALAD
Chinese

1 package bean sprouts
1 can (15-20) water chestnuts,
  well drained and quartered

Mix well and marinate in:
4 tablespoons white vinegar
4 tablespoons sesame oil

4 teaspoons sugar
2 tablespoons light soy sauce

Chill until served.

Volunteer
Cattaraugus County

CUCUMBER SALAD
("Gurken Salat")
German

2 fresh cucumbers
3 tablespoons olive oil or
    ½ cup sour cream
2 tablespoons vinegar

1 tablespoon water
Parsley
Salt and Pepper
Small onion, chopped (optional)

Peel cucumbers and slice very thin. Add and blend oil or cream. Add vinegar, water, parsley and onion immediately before serving.

Mrs. Inge Hinman
Franklin County

COOKED SALAD DRESSING
Pennsylvania Dutch

3 slices bacon
1 egg
4 tablespoons sugar
1 rounded tablespoon flour
¼ teaspoon salt

3 tablespoons vinegar
3 tablespoons water
½ cup water
Lettuce

In medium fry pan fry bacon. Remove bacon and set aside. Mix together egg, sugar, flour and salt. Add 3 tablespoons vinegar and 3 tablespoons water and mix well. Add ½ cup water, stir, and pour gently into warm bacon grease in fry pan. Stir and cook until thick and bubbly. More sugar may be added if a sweeter sauce is desired. In large salad bowl tear lettuce into bite size pieces to make 4 cups. Pour hot dressing over and stir to coat pieces. Crumble cooked bacon over top and serve. Serves 4-6.

Mrs. Evelyn Lang
Orange County

HAWAIIAN MACARONI SALAD
Hawaiian

1 pound Mariana Macaroni
   No.37
3 tablespoons flour
¾ cup sugar
2 eggs
2 medium size cans chunk
   pineapple, drained, save juice

1 large can mandarin oranges,
   drained, save juice
1 jar maraschino cherries,
   drained
1 medium size Cool Whip

Cook macaroni. Drain well, rinse in cold water and drain again. Blend flour and sugar. Beat eggs. Add dry ingredients, then pineapple juice and mandarin juice. Cook until thick. Add oranges and macaroni. Chill overnight. Fold in Cool Whip and cut fruit. Let stand about 4 hours in refrigerator.

Barbara Miller
Erie County

Soups

The Leatherstocking Saga

JAMES FENIMORE COOPER, FOUNDER

James Fenimore Cooper grew up in Cooperstown, New York, a frontier village on the Susquehanna River, which was founded in 1785 by his father, a wealthy Quaker and Federalist member of Congress.

Cooper married a daughter of a wealthy landowning family and settled into the life of a country gentleman. At the age of 30 in response to certain financial reverses but also, according to legend, to his wife's challenge of his claim that he could write a better novel than the popular English one she was reading, he began his literary career.

Cooper traveled to Europe in 1826 and remained for seven years. Returning to Cooperstown in 1833, he found himself at odds with the mood of the country. Finding the Jacksonian democracy highly distasteful, he vented his thoughts in two novels. He became the target of a torrent of public abuse. He responded with a series of libel suits and the fact that he won most of them helped to establish rules of libel in U.S. courts. This made him nearly as well known for litigiousness as for literature and did very little to endear him to his countrymen.

By far his best works, and his greatest contribution to American literature were those comprising the "Leatherstocking Tales."

LEBERKNOEDELSUPPE
(Liver Dumpling Soup)
German

1 pound beef liver, cut into
   chunks
1 large onion, chopped
4 tablespoons lemon juice
1 cup herb seasoned bread
   stuffing
1 cup bread crumbs, made from
   leftover bread, preferably
   whole wheat or rye, a bagel
   works well too.

1 egg
1 teaspoon salt
1 tablespoon parsley flakes
1 teaspoon marjoram
¼ teaspoon ground pepper

Broth
1 bouillon cube

½ cup celery, chopped

Grind up liver in blender together with the chopped onion and the lemon juice. Mix in a large bowl with remaining ingredients. The mixture should be quite soft. Bring water to a boil in a 3 or 4 quart pot. Add bouillon cube and celery. Drop the liver dumpling mixture by the teaspoonful into the boiling broth. The dumplings will float back up to the top. Simmer gently for 20 minutes and serve. Serves 6-8 and goes well with a salad and fresh, whole grain bread.

Helga Stamp
Steuben County

KNEIDLACH
(To be used with soup)
Jewish

3 eggs, separated
¾ cup matzo meal

½ teaspoon salt

Beat egg whites until stiff. Add yolks and continue beating. Fold in matzo meal and salt. Let stand 5 minutes. Wet hands and form into small balls. Drop into boiling salted water in large pot. They will sink to bottom of pot and then rise to top. Cover and cook at slow boil for 20 minutes. To be used in clear chicken soup. Serves 4-6.

Libby Akulin
Otsego County

FARINA DUMPLING SOUP
German

Broth:

3 quarts water
3 pieces chicken
1 soup bone
2 teaspoons salt

1 bay leaf
1 carrot
1 small onion
Parsley

Dumplings:

½ cup milk
⅓ cup Farina
2 teaspoons butter or margarine
Pinch of salt

2 eggs
1 tablespoon flour
3 tablespoons margarine
Nutmeg (sprinkle)

Broth—Boil all above listed ingredients 1½-2 hours. Meanwhile make dumplings. *Dumplings*—In medium saucepan cook milk, Farina, butter and salt. When thick, remove from stove and mix in one egg. Set aside to cool. Then add second egg, flour and nutmeg. Heat 3 tablespoons margarine in frying pan, drop in small "dumplings" with teaspoon and brown lightly on both sides, lift out and drop into boiling broth—simmer 10 minutes.

Mrs. Hans Moeller
Wyoming County

POTATO AND DUMPLING SOUP
Slavic

3 cups flour
3 eggs
½ teaspoon salt
1 cup water
1 can (32 ounces) tomato juice

1 medium onion, diced
¼ pound margarine
2 large potatoes, diced
2 quarts water

In a large bowl, combine flour, eggs and salt and mix well. Add water a little at a time while mixing to make a thick batter. (You may need more or less than 1 cup water depending on the size of the eggs). Bring 2 quarts water to a boil in a large pot and add tomato juice, onion, margarine and potatoes and cook until potatoes begin to soften. Spread thick batter on a plate and drop by the spoonful into the boiling soup. The dumplings will puff and rise to the top. Cover and simmer 5 minutes.

Patricia Varveri
Putnam County

RUSSIAN CABBAGE SOUP
Russian

3-4 pounds cabbage, shredded
2 medium onions, chopped
¼ pound margarine
3 tablespoons flour
4-5 cups of beef stock
2 cups canned tomatoes

2 teaspoons salt
¼ teaspoon pepper
2 tablespoons sugar
2 tablespoons lemon juice
1 teaspoon caraway seeds

In a large soup pot, cook cabbage and onions in margarine for 15-20 minutes. Sprinkle with flour and gradually add stock, stirring constantly until a boil is reached. Add remaining ingredients. Cover and cook 1-1½ hours. Season to taste.

Helen D'Angelo
Dutchess County

VICHYSOISSE
French

4 potatoes, diced
4 leeks, chopped
1 onion, diced
2 tablespoons sweet butter
3 cups consommé

1 teaspoon salt
1 cup milk
2 cups cream
4 tablespoons chives, chopped

Lightly brown white part of leeks and onion in butter. Add potatoes and consommé. Season with salt and bring to boiling point, then allow to simmer until vegetables are tender. Pass vegetables through sieve or put in blender. Blend in milk, then add cream. Add chives. Serve chilled. Serves 6.

Volunteer
Schuyler County

ONION SOUP
Italian

4 to 5 cups onion, chopped
4 ounces butter
2 cups fresh beef stock
⅔ cup tomato purée
⅓ cup flour
⅔ cup medium sherry wine

1 teaspoon garlic powder
1 teaspoon pepper
1-2 teaspoons sugar
Salt to taste
Crusty Italian bread
Mozzarella cheese

Sauté onions slowly in the butter until well browned. Add beef stock. Simmer one hour. Combine in a blender the purée, flour, wine, garlic powder, pepper, sugar, and salt. Blend until smooth. Add slowly to onion mixture, stirring constantly. Simmer one hour. Taste and adjust seasonings. Serve in individual cups or soup tureen. Just before serving, place a slice of crusty Italian bread on soup and cover with Mozzarella cheese. Place in 375 degree oven until cheese melts, or in microwave oven for one minute on high.

Note: 2 bouillon cubes or Campbell's beef soup mixed according to directions may be used. If other than fresh beef stock is used, taste before adding salt. This onion soup was very much in demand at a restaurant I once owned.

Jolene Micoli
Niagara County

RED KIDNEY BEAN SOUP
Portuguese

¼ pound salt pork, diced
1 onion, chopped
½ pound linguica or chourico
  sausage, diced
1 pound squash (any type),
  diced

Salt and pepper
1 pound red kidney beans,
  soaked overnight
4 medium white potatoes, sliced

Fry pork until golden. Add onion and sausage, fry 5 minutes. Add the potatoes and squash with beans and seasonings. Cover with water and simmer until beans are tender, about ½ hour.

Viola M. Lasher
Fulton County

SOUR-CREAM PEACH SOUP
Polish

2 #303 cans peaches, sliced
1¾ cups peach juice and cold
  water
1 tablespoon cornstarch

1 teaspoon lemon juice
⅔ cup sour cream
½ teaspoon cinnamon

Drain peaches, reserve liquid. Pureé peaches. Set aside. Measure drained peach liquid. Add enough cold water to equal 1¾ cups liquid. Thicken ¼ cup peach juice and water with cornstarch. Add thickened juice to remaining liquid. Heat until thickened, about 10 minutes. Stir in lemon juice. Add pureéd peaches and sour cream; blend well. Serve immediately. Garnish with cinnamon. Serves 4.

Volunteer
Hamilton County

GULYAS SOUP
A hearty beef soup
Hungarian

2 tablespoons lard
1 pound stewing beef
2 medium onions, chopped
1 clove garlic, finely chopped
2 teaspoons paprika
3 cups beef stock or broth
2 cups water
½ teaspoon caraway seeds
½ teaspoon marjoram,
  crumbled

Salt and pepper to taste
1 16-ounce can tomatoes,
  broken up
2 medium potatoes, diced
2 medium carrots, sliced
2 green peppers, cut up in
  chunks
2 tablespoons flour
2 tablespoons water
Sour cream, optional

Melt lard in frying pan and add cut up stewing beef. Brown well on all sides. Remove meat from frying pan and reserve. Add onions and garlic to frying pan and cook for 4 minutes, stirring occasionally. Place all of the above ingredients in a large saucepan and add paprika, beef stock, 2 cups water, caraway seeds, marjoram, salt, pepper and reserved meat. Stir well and bring to a boil over moderate heat. Reduce heat to low and cook covered for 45 minutes. Add tomatoes, potatoes, carrots and green peppers. Stir well and return to a boil. Cover and cook for 30 minutes. Combine flour and 2 tablespoons water to make a smooth paste. Add slowly to soup, stirring well. Cook over low heat, stirring until thickened. Serve soup in individual bowls and top with sour cream if desired.

Sister Mary Johanna Ryan, R.N., E.T
Montgomery County

PANSIT DE MOLO
Philippines

Part I
Prepare the filling:
1 cup beef or pork, ground
½ teaspoon parsley, dried
1 clove garlic, pounded &
   chopped fine

2 eggs
Soy sauce
Salt and pepper

Mix all the above ingredients thoroughly, and set aside.

Part II
1 pound wonton wrappers

Note: Wonton wrappers may be obtained from an Oriental Market.

Cut wonton wrappers into triangles. Wrap a teaspoonful of the meat mixture in the wonton wrapper.

Part III
2 chicken breasts
15 medium size shrimps, sliced
   into halves or quarters
2 tablespoons oil
1 clove garlic, sliced

1 medium onion
Soy sauce
Salt, pepper
Accent

Wash and boil chicken breasts until tender with salt and pepper. Strain the broth. Flake the chicken and slice the shrimps into halves or quarters. Sauté garlic and onions in oil. Then add the flaked chicken and sliced shrimps. Pour a good quantity of the chicken stock and allow to boil for 5 minutes. Then add the wrapped Pansit and allow to boil for 15 minutes. Add soy sauce, salt, pepper, and Accent to taste. Serve hot.

Pacita G. Cabaluna
Franklin County

FISH CHOWDER
English

1 4-5 pound whole haddock
1½ quarts boiling water
2 teaspoons salt
1½ pounds potatoes, peeled
  and diced
¼ pound salt pork, diced
1 medium-sized onion, thinly
  sliced

1 tablespoon flour
⅛ teaspoon Worcesterhire
  sauce
1 cup milk
1 cup light cream
Salt and pepper to taste
Chopped parsley

Clean fish thoroughly; do not remove head. Cover fish with the boiling water; add 2 teaspoons salt. Cover and simmer gently 1 hour. Remove fish and cool. Strain broth; add potatoes and cook about 20 minutes until just tender. In a heavy saucepan over low heat cook salt pork until lightly browned; add onion and cook until tender. Sprinkle flour and Worcestershire sauce over salt pork, onions and stir to blend. Drain liquid from the potatoes and gradually stir the liquid into the flour mixture. Cook and stir until smooth and slightly thickened. Stir in milk and cream. Remove head, bones and skin from fish and coarsley flake the fish. Add the potatoes and fish to the chowder and heat thoroughly but do not boil. Season to taste with salt and pepper. Sprinkle with parsley. Serves 5.

Volunteer
Allegany County

CIORBA TARANESCA
Rumanian

1 small chicken, or 2-pound
  veal or beef
2 onions, sliced
1 large carrot
A few celery leaves, chopped
A little lovage (optional)

3-4 tomatoes
Pinch of red pepper
1 teaspoon parsley, chopped
Salt and pepper
1 pint water
A sprig of thyme

Cut the meat, or the chicken, into small pieces. Put in a pan with cold water and let it come to a boil. Skim well. Add salt, vegetables, red pepper and lovage. Boil for two hours. Add more water, if necessary. Sprinkle the chopped parsley and the sprig of thyme over the top when ready to serve. Serves 4-5.

Volunteer
Herkimer County

CHICKEN SOUP
Jewish

1 plump chicken	2 parsnips
2 onions (peeled)	Fresh dill
6 carrots, sliced	Fresh parsley
4 stalks celery	Salt and pepper

Cut chicken in ⅛'s, clean and put in large pot with neck, gizzard and onions. Cover with cold water and bring to a boil uncovered. Skim top with spoon until clear. Add sliced carrots, celery, and parsnips. Add fresh parsley and dill which are first tied with string. Add salt and pepper to taste. Simmer covered for 2½-3 hours or until broth is golden and chicken is soft. Remove celery, parsnips, onions, parsley, dill and discard. Remove chicken and you have soup and carrots. Serve with noodles or matzo balls.

Mrs. Harold Nodelman
Columbia County

MANASTADA
Italian

Ham bone or sausage	Spinach or swiss chard
2 quarts water	Corn
Salt	Navy beans
Pepper	Italian beans
Oregano	Ditalini macaroni
Parsley	Yellow or green string beans
Sweet basil	(optional)

Brown meat in large saucepan. Add water, salt, pepper, oregano, parsley, and sweet basil. Chop spinach or swiss chard and add to water. Add corn, navy beans, and Italian beans. Simmer covered for 30 minutes. Stir in macaroni thoroughly. Simmer for another 20 minutes, stirring occasionally. Yellow or green string beans may also be added.

Note: This recipe is usually made with left-overs. Quantities depend on how much is left from a previous meal or how thick you wish it to be. Manastada can easily be a meal in itself and is very inexpensive to make not to mention simple and delicious. Tastes best on a cool day with a fresh loaf of Italian bread.

Tony Passalacqua
Yates County

Vegetables

The Universal Friend

JEMIMA WILKINSON, FOUNDER

In 1790 the population of Yates County was listed as 388 pioneers among whom Jemima Wilkinson endures as the best known personality.

Jemima became ill at the age of 23 of a disease that defied medical diagnosis. She went into a trance, and for thirty-six hours appeared to be lifeless. She then suddenly recovered, called for her clothes, dressed and walked about. She disclaimed the personality of Jemima Wilkinson but proclaimed herself to be the Public Universal Friend.

It is said that Jemima Wilkinson was the first woman to form an American Religious Society. Looking for a New Jerusalem, she and her religious followers, of about 260 persons, traveled to the south end of Seneca Lake. Here her disciples erected a log meeting house and a dwelling house for her. It should be noted that the Indians looked upon her with much favor, which was in direct contrast with their general hostility toward most other whites. They addressed her as a "great woman preacher" (Squaw Shin-ne-waw-na gis-taw-ge) and they kept the Friend's larder well supplied with venison and other foods.

BROCCOLI SUPREME
French

2 packages frozen broccoli
  spears (10 ounces each)
Salt and pepper to taste
1 can (10½ ounces) condensed
  cream of chicken soup
½ cup mayonnaise

Juice of one lemon
Parmesan cheese, grated
Bread crumbs
2 tablespoons butter or
  margarine, melted

Cook broccoli spears just until tender, drain. Place in medium casserole dish and season to taste with salt and pepper. Combine soup, mayonnaise and lemon juice. Pour over broccoli and gently mix together. Mix melted butter with desired amount of breadcrumbs and add to broccoli mixture. Top with Parmesan cheese. Bake at 350 degrees for 30 minutes. Serves 4-6.

Note: For a very simple Chicken Divan dinner, I add chicken to this recipe.

Carol King
Seneca County

SOUR-SWEET CARROTS
German

2 pounds hot cooked carrots
  (still firm)

1 onion, sliced
1 green pepper, sliced thin

Sauce (Mix the following)
1 can tomato soup
¾ cup vinegar
1 tablespoon Worcestershire
  sauce

1 teaspoon mustard
1 cup sugar
Salt and pepper

Cook carrots for 10 minutes in water at simmering temperature. Remove and drain well. Place in casserole dish and mix sauce in the order of ingredients listed. Pour over carrots, cover and let set overnight.

Note: This will keep several days.

Virginia D. Ellis
Allegany County

CARROT TZIMMES
Jewish

8 carrots ¾-inch thick
½ cup water
3 sweet potatoes
⅓ cup honey

1 tablespoon lemon juice
1 tablespoon margarine
½ teaspoon salt

In heavy saucepan cook carrots covered with water until almost tender. Cut sweet potatoes in quarters, cook for another 15 minutes. Stir in honey, lemon juice, margarine and salt. If gravy is not sweet enough, add 1 tablespoon brown sugar and bake in 350 degree oven for 35 to 40 minutes or until potatoes are soft. You can add prunes, cooked and pitted the last 15 minutes, if desired.

Mrs. David L. Frisch
Fulton County

CAULIFLOWER ALA POLAND
Polish

2 hard-cooked egg yolks
1 teaspoon dried parsley flakes
2 tablespoons sour cream
¼ teaspoon white pepper

1 head cauliflower
1 teaspoon salt
¼ cup butter
3 tablespoons bread crumbs

Mash egg yolks in a small bowl. Add parsley flakes, sour cream, and white pepper to egg yolks. Blend. Reserve for later. Wash cauliflower head; remove outside leaves. Select a saucepan large enough to accommodate the head of cauliflower. Cover bottom of pan with 1-2 inches of water. Add salt to water; bring to rapid boil. Add cauliflower to saucepan; cover. Boil cauliflower 25 minutes or until fork-tender. Drain immediately. Melt butter; stir in bread crumbs. Pour buttered bread crumbs over cauliflower; garnish with reserved egg-yolk mixture. Serves 8.

Volunteer
Lewis County

STUFFED EGGPLANT
Israeli

1 medium eggplant
1 small onion, chopped
1 clove garlic, minced
1 tablespoon oregano
1 egg, beaten
2 tablespoons olive oil, or other
  salad oil

½ cup (4 ounces) bread crumbs
Pinch of salt
2 tablespoons fresh or dried
  parsley, chopped
Grated cheese (optional)

Bake the eggplant whole in a flat pan for 30-45 minutes at 350 degrees. Then cut the eggplant in half lengthwise. Scoop out the inside part, including the seeds, if any, and put into a small bowl with the beaten egg and the bread crumbs. Sauté the chopped onion and garlic in the oil in a small skillet, add the oregano, salt and parsley when the onion looks translucent. Remove from stove, and mix into the eggplant. Fill the two eggplant halves with this mixture, place on a flat baking pan or in a metal pan with low sides, place the stuffed eggplant under the broiler and broil for about 15 minutes. Cheese (either grated by hand or commercially grated) may be added to the stuffing but it is best to mix it into the eggplant before filling the shells, to avoid having the cheese scorched under the broiler.

Note: I was introduced to this tasty dish at a meal prepared by friends in Jerusalem, Israel. It was served (without cheese) along with a Sabbath meat meal, as a side dish, with a salad and other fresh vegetables and fruits for dessert.

Suzanne Hecht
Tompkins County

FRENCH-FRIED EGGPLANT
Polish

1 medium eggplant
1 cup all-purpose white flour
½ teaspoon salt
¼ teaspoon black pepper

1 egg, beaten
½ cup milk
1 cup bread crumbs

Peel eggplant; cut into ¾-inch strips. Combine flour and spices in shallow bowl. Combine egg and milk in another shallow bowl. Pour bread crumbs into a third shallow bowl. Dip eggplant strips in seasoned flour, then in egg mixture; shake, then dip into crumbs and shake again. Fry breaded strips in oil heated to 375 degrees for 4 minutes, turning them once during cooking period. Drain on a brown paper bag. Serves 4.

Volunteer
Livingston County

POTATO PANCAKES
(Latkes)
Jewish

6 medium potatoes
1 large onion
2 eggs
½ cup flour

1 teaspoon salt
⅛ teaspoon black pepper
Vegetable shortening or oil for
    deep frying

Pare and grate potatoes into large mixing bowl. Squeeze out liquid. Peel and grate onion into potatoes. Add eggs, flour, salt and pepper. Stir to make a smooth batter that will drop heavily from the spoon. Heat the shortening (or oil) in a heavy frying pan using enough to cover pancakes amply. Drop the batter from spoon into hot shortening, making pancakes 3-inches in diameter. Fry over moderate heat until brown on underside, turn to brown. Lift out and drain excess oil on paper towel. Pancakes should be puffed and brown. Serves 4-6.

Note: Serve with applesauce or sour cream.

Claire Greenfogel
Montgomery County

ALICHA
Afro-American

SPICE BUTTER

½ pound butter	Dash white pepper
1 tablespoon onion, chopped	Dash black pepper
1 large toe garlic, finely chopped	⅛ teaspoon ginger
¼ teaspoon curry powder	1-2 cardamom seeds (insides only)
¼ teaspoon dry mustard	¼ teaspoon oregano

Melt butter, add remainder of ingredients and simmer 45 minutes. Let settle.

2-3 medium onions	1 pound stew meat, chopped
1 small toe garlic, minced	1 large head cabbage
1 teaspoon salad oil	¼ pound green beans, (optional)
¼ teaspoon curry powder	1 tablespoon spice butter
2 large carrots	
3-4 medium potatoes	

Prepare spice butter first. While spice butter is simmering, cut up onions, garlic, carrots, potatoes, meat, cabbage and beans (if used). Using a 4-6 quart covered dutch oven, put in onions, garlic, salad oil, curry powder and spice butter, add ¼ cup water, cover and simmer for 30 minutes, stirring frequently. Add stew meat and simmer 15-20 minutes. Next add carrots, potatoes and beans plus a couple tablespoons of water if necessary and cook approximately 15 minutes. (Vegetables will be only half cooked at this point). Finally add ½ cup water and chopped cabbage and simmer 10 minutes or until cabbage is done. This makes 5-6 servings.

Note: Spice butter can be used on any vegetable desired to add a delightful and different taste. May be used for frying meats or fish.

Agazi Bereket-Ab
Saratoga County

Microwave
POTATOES DAUPHINOIS
French

2 pounds long white baking
  potatoes
1½-ounces butter
½ teaspoon sea salt
¼ teaspoon ground white
  pepper, freshly ground

2 cups milk
1½ cups Creme Fraische
  (freshly made)

Creme Fraische:
Combine 1 tablespoon buttermilk and 1 cup heavy cream. Keep at 80 degrees for 12 hours.

Peel potatoes, slice into medallions ⅛-inch thick, submerge in ice cold water until all are sliced. Dry carefully and arrange randomly in casserole sprayed with Pam. Do not mound potatoes. During layering, sprinkle bits of butter, salt and pepper until all are used. Pour sufficient milk over potatoes until they are covered. Place casserole in microwave oven, uncovered at high heat for 17 minutes or until potatoes are soft and most of milk has been absorbed. Pour off any remaining milk. Replace in microwave at 50 degrees for 3 minutes or until potatoes are dried. Remove and ladle Creme Fraische into casserole and allow to settle and flow about potatoes. Return to microwave at high heat for 8 minutes until creme is thickened and slight crust or skin forms. Dish can be held at room temperature for several hours if desired. Place in conventional oven at 350 degrees for 10 minutes, if directly from microwave. Add 5 minutes if held at room temperature. Serve with dry, hearty white burgundy.

Philip Ikins, MD
Onondaga County

POTATO DUMPLINGS
(KARTOFLANE KLUSKI)
Polish

2 cups hot potatoes, mashed
⅓ cup fine dry bread crumbs
2 egg yolks
¾ teaspoon salt

¼ teaspoon pepper
⅓ cup all-purpose flour
2 egg whites, beaten stiff, but
not dry

Mix ingredients in a large bowl in the order given. Place on a floured board and roll to pencil thickness. Cut into 2 or 3-inch strips. Drop into BOILING SALT WATER . Cook until dumplings float to the top. Croquettes: Sauté ½ cup chopped onion in 2 tablespoons butter. Proceed as in recipe for potato dumplings, add onions to potatoes. Roll strips in fine dry bread-crumbs. Pan fry in butter until golden brown.

Note: Serve in place of potatoes or noodles, great with pork and hot gravy.

Anne Koslosky
Oneida County

PILAF WITH NUTS
Greek

2 tablespoons butter
¼ cup pine nuts
¼ cup slivered almonds

1 cup long-grain rice
1 teaspoon salt
2½ cups chicken broth

Melt butter in a heavy saucepan over medium heat. Add nuts. Sauté until lightly browned. Stir in rice and salt. Sauté, stirring constantly, until butter is light amber and foams. Stir in broth. Bring to boil. Cover. Simmer 25 minutes or until rice is tender and liquid absorbed. Let stand, covered, 15 minutes before serving. Serves 4.

Volunteer
Orange County

SPINACH PIE
(Spanakopita)
Greek

3 packages frozen spinach,
chopped (10-ounces per
package)
1 medium onion, chopped
1 pound Greek feta cheese,
crumbled

8 eggs
1 pound butter, melted
1 pound Filo dough (pastry
sheets)
Salt and pepper to taste

Note: Filo dough may be found in Greek or Italian grocery stores.

Thaw spinach and use cheesecloth to squeeze out all liquid. Mix with chopped onions, crumbled cheese, eggs, salt and pepper in a large bowl. Pour half of the melted butter over the mixture and toss lightly to combine all ingredients. Brush the bottom and sides of a 9 x 13-inch pan. Lay six pastry sheets into pan, brushing each layer with melted butter. Spread half of the spinach mixture on pastry sheet. Repeat this process, ending with six top layers. Brush top with butter. With a sharp knife dipped in hot water, cut the pie into twelve squares. Bake at 350 degrees for one hour. Serves 12.

Helen Jon Collins
Columbia County

CANDIED YAMS WITH BRANDY
Afro-American

6 medium yams, washed
thoroughly
1 cup sugar
3 tablespoons butter
¼ cup lemon juice

¼ cup water
1 teaspoon nutmeg
1 teaspoon cinnamon
Salt
¼ cup brandy

Cut the 6 yams lengthwise and arrange in casserole. Mix together the sugar, butter, water, lemon juice, nutmeg and cinnamon. Sprinkle with salt. Pour mixture over yams and add ¼ cup brandy. Cover and bake in moderate oven (350 degrees) for 30 minutes. Uncover and brown for 15 minutes.

Anne Brown
Chemung County

YAMS AND SAUSAGE CREOLE
American Creole

5 tablespoons butter, softened
2 pounds yams
1½ cups soft fresh crumbs made from French or Italian type white bread, pulverized in blender
½ pound fresh pork sausage meat, (the breakfast sausage variety)

½ cup onions, finely chopped
½ cup celery, finely chopped
½ teaspoon poultry seasoning
¼ teaspoon salt
¼ teaspoon black pepper, ground

Preheat the oven to 375 degrees. With pastry brush, spread the tablespoon of softened butter evenly over bottom and sides of a 1½ quart baking dish. Set aside. Drop yams into boiling water. Water is to cover yams completely. Cook briskly, uncovered, for about 20 minutes or till yams pierce easily with a fork. Drain and peel. Purée yams through potato ricer or mash until smooth with the back of a fork. Place in a bowl. In a heavy 10-12-inch skillet, melt remaining 4 tablespoons butter over moderate heat. Add bread crumbs; stirring often, fry until crisp and brown. With slotted spoon, transfer to bowl. Add sausage meat to fat left in skillet, cook at moderate heat, mashing meat to eliminate lumps until there is no trace of pink left. Add meat to bowl with slotted spoon. Pour off fat leaving thin film of fat in skillet, add onions and celery. Cook for about five minutes over moderate heat until soft but not brown. Scrape contents of skillet into bowl of sausage and crumbs. Add puréed yams, poultry seasoning, salt and pepper, stir until well mixed. Taste for seasoning. Transfer to butter dish, spread evenly smoothing top with fork. Bake in middle of oven about 25 minutes until golden brown and crusty. Serve at once directly from baking dish. Serves 6.

Mrs. Rodney W. Conrad, Jr.
Niagara County

BORDELAISE SAUCE
French

2 onions, chopped
½ cup red wine
1 cup brown sauce

2 tablespoons beef marrow
½ teaspoon parsley, chopped

Cook onions in red wine until reduced to almost ¼ orginal amount, add brown sauce and boil slowly for approximately 10 minutes. Dice beef marrow and poach in salted boiling water for 2 minutes. Drain, add chopped parsley and marrow before serving.

Volunteer
Cortland County

HOLLANDAISE SAUCE
French

8 tablespoons butter
 (¼ pound)
4 egg yolks

2 teaspoons lemon juice
Salt and pepper to taste

Divide butter in 3 parts. Place egg yolks and 1 part of butter in top of double boiler. Stir rapidly over hot water until butter is melted, then add second portion of butter and as it melts add third portion, stirring continually. Do not allow water in bottom of boiler to come to a boil. When butter is entirely melted, remove pan from heat and continue beating for a few more minutes, add lemon juice, salt and pepper. Replace pan over hot water and beat for 1 or 2 minutes.

Note: Excellent served over vegetables such as asparagus, broccoli, etc.

Volunteer
Niagara County

Chef's Collection

Featuring Pasquale (Pat) Rocco, Executive Chef and Colleagues

Chef's Collection

Pasquale (Pat) Rocco, Executive Chef is an elected member of the American Academy of Chef's and is a Member of American Institute of Chef's (Who's Who in Food). Pat Rocco has travelled extensively around the country to schools, colleges, community and civic groups giving lectures, demonstrations and slide presentations of his culinary art.

Many awards, medals and honors have been bestowed upon this world renown chef, to name just a few:

    First prize winner ten years in New York International Food Show,
        sponsored by the Societé Culinaire Philanthropique
    Silver Medal, World Culinary Olympics, Frankfurt Germany
    Gold Medal, American Academy of Chef's
    Bronze Medal, Societé Culinaire Philanthropique, French Organization
    Auguste Escoffier, Gold Medal
    Silver Medal, La Saint-Michel Academy of France
    Gold Medal, Otto Gensh, French
    Gold Medal, International Chef's Association
    Canadian Gold Medal, and was
    Voted Chef of the Year 1973-74.

In Mr. Rocco's travels he has been a chef for Zsa Zsa Gabor, Van Johnson, Milton Berle, Anthony Quinn, Governor Malcolm Wilson, Governor Nelson Rockefeller, Governor Hugh Carey, and Mary Lou Whitney.

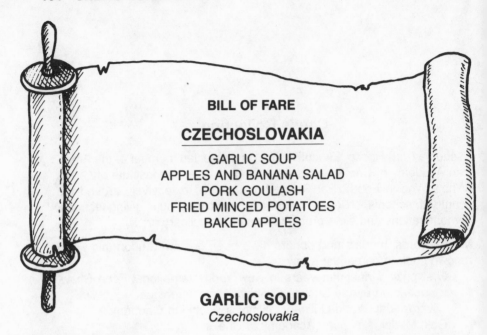

BILL OF FARE

CZECHOSLOVAKIA

GARLIC SOUP
APPLES AND BANANA SALAD
PORK GOULASH
FRIED MINCED POTATOES
BAKED APPLES

GARLIC SOUP
Czechoslovakia

2½ quarts beef stock
Salt and pepper
Pinch of thyme
3 eggs, beaten

2 tablespoons garlic, minced
6 slices dark bread
½ cup oil

Season stock with salt and pepper and flavor with a little thyme. Add eggs and garlic and bring to boil. Make bread cubes and fry in oil. Toss over soup when serving.

Pasquale (Pat) Rocco
Albany County

APPLES AND BANANA SALAD
Czechoslovakia

4 ounces apples, peeled and
cut into strips
¾ cup bananas, cut in oval
slices

¼ pint heavy cream, whipped
2 lemons

Cut apples into strips and bananas into oval slices. Flavor the cream with lemon juice and mix with apples and bananas. Refrigerate at least two hours before serving.

Pasquale (Pat) Rocco
Albany County

PORK GOULASH
Czechoslovakia

1½ pounds shoulder of pork,
  cut into cubes
6 tablespoons oil
½ cup onions, chopped

4 tablespoons mushrooms
Salt and pepper to taste
Pinch of marjoram

Cook pork slowly in hot oil with chopped onions and mushrooms, adding salt and pepper and a little marjoram. Add a little water to keep meat nice and moist. Cook until meat is fork tender. Boiled or roasted potatoes can be served with this dish.

Pasquale (Pat) Rocco

FRIED MINCED POTATOES
Czechoslovakia

2 pounds raw potatoes
3 eggs
½ cup milk
¾ cup flour

Salt and pepper
Pinch of thyme
Minced garlic
½ cup oil

Mince raw potatoes and pat dry with paper towel. Add beaten eggs, milk and flour. Fold to make a thick mixture. Add salt, pepper, thyme and minced garlic. Put oil in skillet to get hot. With a tablespoon, drop mixture in hot oil 2 inches apart. Turn over to make both sides golden brown.

Pasquale (Pat) Rocco

BAKED APPLES
Czechoslovakia

10 apples
¾ cups plus 2 tablespoons
  butter
3 tablespoons sugar

¾ cup plus 2 tablespoons
  walnuts, chopped
½ pint cream, whipped

Core apples. Stand them in a buttered fireproof dish, pour melted butter over and bake until cooked but still firm. Sprinkle with sugar, allow to cool and top with whipped cream and chopped walnuts.

Pasquale (Pat) Rocco

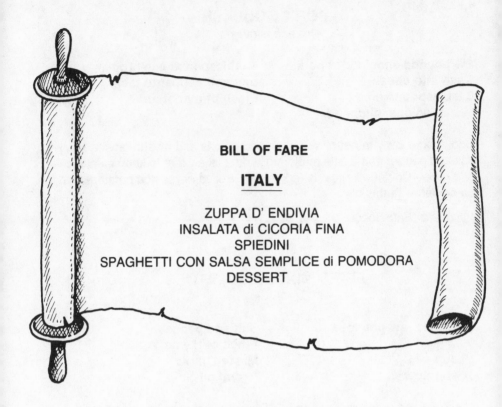

BILL OF FARE

ITALY

ZUPPA D' ENDIVIA
INSALATA di CICORIA FINA
SPIEDINI
SPAGHETTI CON SALSA SEMPLICE di POMODORA
DESSERT

ZUPPA D'ENDIVIA
(ENDIVE FRIED IN BUTTER)
Italy

1 head endive, soaked, rinsed, thoroughly drained and chopped
3 tablespoons olive oil
2 cloves garlic, split into 4 strips

¼ cup onion, chopped
1 teaspoon basil
8 cups chicken broth
Salt and pepper to taste

Set endive aside. In a saucepan, heat oil, sauté garlic very lightly, add onions, stir well, add basil. When onions are transparent, add endive. Stir well and sauté until endive is limp. (Don't scorch the garlic and onions). Add chicken broth, bring to boil, turn heat down to simmer, add seasonings. Simmer on low heat for 20-25 minutes.

Pasquale (Pat) Rocco
Albany County

INSALATA di Cicoria Fina
(Dandelion Salad)
Italy

1 pound dandelion greens,
  washed, drained and cut into
  2-inch pieces
4 tablespoons olive oil

12 ripe olives (optional)
1 garlic clove
2 tablespoons wine vinegar
Salt and pepper to taste

Dry dandelions on absorbent towel and chill in refrigerator for about 10 minutes. Rub wooden salad bowl with clove of garlic. Place chilled dandelions in bowl and pour vinegar and oil over leaves. Add salt and pepper to taste. Add olives and mix well.

Pasquale (Pat) Rocco

SPIEDINI
Italy

24 ounces lean veal, cut
  into 12 cubes
4 onions, quartered
2 large tomatoes, quartered
4 large mushroom caps
  (stems removed)

4 links Italian sausage
4 strips of very lean bacon
Wine vinegar
Olive oil
Salt and pepper to taste

On a long skewer, slide on a veal cube, 1 quartered tomato, two slices of onion, 1 link of sausage, lengthwise, strip of bacon, folded, 1 mushroom cap, 1 veal cube, 1 quartered tomato, and two slices onion. Repeat process to fill 4 skewers. Brush with wine vinegar, and olive oil. Sprinkle with salt and pepper. Put in a pan, place in hot oven 20-25 minutes. Turn skewers over at least once. Serve with Pasta.

Pasquale (Pat) Rocco

SPAGHETTI CON SALSA SEMPLICE DI POMODORO
(Spaghetti with Plain Tomato Sauce)
Italy

4 tablespoons olive oil
2 cloves garlic
½ teaspoon basil
½ teaspoon oregano
1 large can tomato purée or
   crushed tomatoes

½ teaspoon sugar (optional)
1 bay leaf
Salt and pepper to taste
1 pound spaghetti
Grated cheese, (Romano,
   Parmesan or combination)

Heat olive oil in saucepan, add garlic and brown lightly with basil and oregano. Add tomatoes, sugar, bay leaf, salt and pepper. Simmer over low heat for about 1 hour, stirring frequently to keep from burning. Cook spaghetti in rapidly boiling water until tender (about 20 minutes). Pour sauce over spaghetti and sprinkle generously with grated cheese.

Pasquale (Pat) Rocco

After dinner (in place of dessert)
Serve:
Sharp cheese—Provolone
Fruit medley—apples, pears,
   grapes, melon, assorted nuts

Italian bread
Expresso coffee

Pasquale (Pat) Rocco

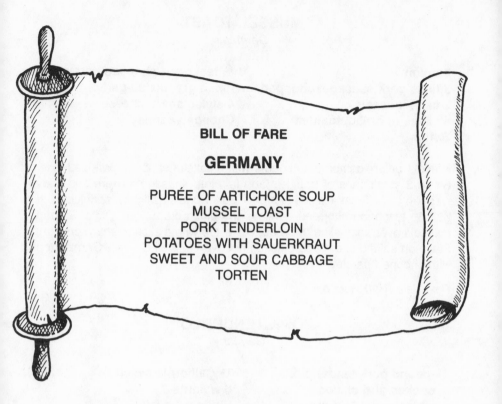

BILL OF FARE

GERMANY

PURÉE OF ARTICHOKE SOUP
MUSSEL TOAST
PORK TENDERLOIN
POTATOES WITH SAUERKRAUT
SWEET AND SOUR CABBAGE
TORTEN

PURÉE OF ARTICHOKE SOUP
Germany

10 fresh artichoke bottoms	**2 pints chicken broth**
½ cup butter	**Pinch of mace and salt**
½ cup plus 2 tablespoons flour	**4 egg yolks**
2½ pints milk	**½ pint dairy cream**

Boil artichoke bottoms until tender. Prepare a roux with butter and flour, gradually add milk and broth, mix thoroughly. Add artichoke bottoms, season with salt, flavor with a little mace and simmer for 30 minutes. Rub through a fine sieve, re-heat and thicken with egg yolks which have been blended with the cream. Adjust seasoning.

Pasquale (Pat) Rocco
Albany County

MUSSEL TOAST
Germany

1 onion
3 links pork sausage, chopped
2 cans mussels
4 slices of bread, toasted
Butter

½ teaspoon chopped parsley
Pinch granulated garlic
4 slices sharp cheese
Chopped parsley

Mince 1 onion, combine and sauté with 3 links of chopped pork sausage. Strain 2 small cans of mussels and fold into sausage mixture and cook just till brown. Toast 4 slices of bread. Butter one side lightly, sprinkle each with ½ teaspoon chopped parsley, and pinch granulated garlic. Spread mussels over each slice of bread, cover top with a slice of sharp cheese. Place on baking sheet and place in hot oven to melt cheese. Garnish top with chopped parsley.

Pasquale (Pat) Rocco

PORK TENDERLOIN
Germany

¼ pound pork tenderloin,
  cooked and chilled
4 tablespoons foie gras
  (chicken livers)

½ California peach
6 walnuts
White wine jelly

Cut six pieces of tenderloins the same size and pipe on foie gras using a pastry bag fitted with a plain tube. Cut peach half into 6 pieces and place one piece of each slice of tenderloin together with a walnut. Top with wine jelly.

Pasquale (Pat) Rocco

POTATOES WITH SAUERKRAUT
Germany

4 medium sized potatoes,
  peeled, quartered, then cut
  each quarter lengthwise

2 tablespoons oil
1 cup sauerkraut
Salt and pepper to taste

Place potatoes in hot oil in skillet. Fry to golden brown. Add sauerkraut evenly over potatoes. Stir well, lower heat and let simmer 10-12 minutes covered, stirring occasionally. Season with salt and pepper.

Pasquale (Pat) Rocco

SWEET AND SOUR RED CABBAGE
Germany

1 medium-sized red cabbage
2 tablespoons oil
1 tablespoon salt
½ medium onion, minced
1 cup unsweetened
  applesauce

Pinch of black pepper
Enough water to just cover
  cabbage in pan
½ cup brown sugar
4 tablespoons flour
¼ cup vinegar

Chop cabbage, put in a pan with hot oil. Stir well. Sprinkle with salt, put in onions and stir constantly for 3 minutes. Add applesauce, pepper and water. Bring to a hard boil, then lower heat to a slow boil. Cook about 45 minutes. Mix together the sugar, flour and vinegar. Fold into cabbage. Keep stirring. Cook 5-7 minutes longer.

Pasquale (Pat) Rocco

TORTEN
Germany

½ cup plus 2 tablespoons egg
  yolks
6 tablespoons confectioners'
  sugar
6 tablespoons almonds,
  chopped
6¼ tablespoons water
Grated lemon peel from 1 small
  lemon

½ cup plus 1 tablespoon egg
  whites
2 tablespoons confectioners'
  sugar
6 tablespoons flour
Lemon fondant

Beat egg yolks with sugar and chopped almonds until foamy. Add water, lemon peel and whip for 15 seconds. Separately whip egg whites with 2 tablespoons sugar to a hard peak and stir gently into first mixture. Fold in the flour. Pour into 2 pans and bake at 350 degrees. When cold split layers and fill with lemon custard and coat with flavored fondant.

Pasquale (Pat) Rocco

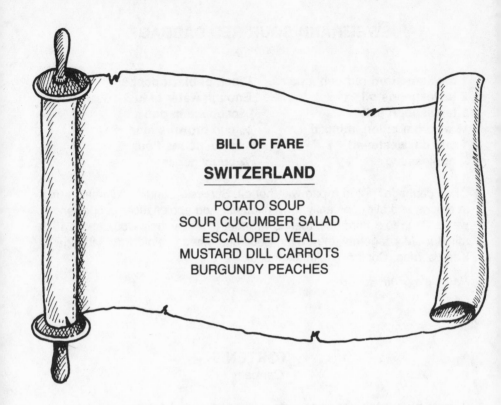

BILL OF FARE

SWITZERLAND

POTATO SOUP
SOUR CUCUMBER SALAD
ESCALOPED VEAL
MUSTARD DILL CARROTS
BURGUNDY PEACHES

POTATO SOUP
Switzerland

¼ cup butter
½ cup onion, finely chopped
1 teaspoon salt (optional)
¼ teaspoon white pepper
3½ cups raw potatoes, diced

2½ cups chicken stock
2 egg yolks, slightly beaten
¼ cup cold milk
1 tablespoon parsley, chopped

Sauté onion in hot butter until soft and clear, add seasoning, potatoes and stock. Let come to a boil and cut heat down to a simmer. Stir well, continue simmering for about 20-30 minutes. Make a roux out of cream and egg yolks. Beat together and pour slowly into potatoes while stirring until you have proper thickness. Adjust seasoning, if needed. Use parsley as garnish.

Pasquale (Pat) Rocco
Albany County

SOUR CUCUMBER SALAD
Switzerland

2 cucumbers
½ cup white vinegar
3 tablespoons water
1½ tablespoons sugar

½ teaspoon salt
Pinch white pepper
1 tablespoon pimiento, chopped

Leave skin on cucumber. Cut each cucumber into eight slices. Place in mixing bowl. Add all remaining ingredients. Stir well and let stand about 1 hour. Serve chilled.

Pasquale (Pat) Rocco

ESCALOPED VEAL
Switzerland

12 pieces of veal, 2-ounces
  each
1-pound Gruyere cheese,
  cut thin
3 medium size firm tomatoes,
  cut thin
6 large eggs, plus 2
  tablespoons of milk

Unflavored breadcrumbs, finely
  crushed
Salt and pepper to taste
  (optional)
6 thin slices of lean ham
1 medium lemon

Pound out the veal, all the same size, then cover 6 pieces of veal, first the cheese, then the tomatoes, ham, and cover again with cheese. Place 6 remaining pieces of veal on top, like a sandwich, beat eggs and milk together to make egg wash. Add seasoning to eggs, then gently take each stack and dust with breadcrumbs, top, bottom and sides, then dip into egg wash, and back into crumbs. Set aside in a tray also dusted with crumbs, until you finish all 6. Combine oil and butter and heat in skillet. Place each veal in skillet gently and simmer. Use the juice of the lemon to flavor, simmer slowly and use butter, oil and lemon juice as flavored sauce. Cook until nice and golden brown.

Pasquale (Pat) Rocco

MUSTARD DILL CARROTS
Switzerland

5 medium carrots, sliced
2 tablespoons oil or butter
¼ cup chicken stock or water

¼ teaspoon salt
1 teaspoon dill weed, chopped
1 tablespoon regular mustard

Boil carrots in stock or water with the oil or butter. Lower heat to simmer about 10 minutes. Keep pan covered while boiling and simmering. Remove cover after 10 minutes and let liquid boil down to just a small amount. Stir in dill weed and mustard together. Stir well. Serve.

Pasquale (Pat) Rocco

BURGUNDY PEACH'S
Switzerland

6 medium peaches
4-ounces fine brown sugar
1 quart of good burgundy
Rind of ⅛ of lemon

Rind of 1 medium orange
1 piece of cinnamon quill (stick)
 ¼-inch long
½ pint of heavy cream

Clean and skin peaches, combine the peaches, sugar, wine, lemon, orange and cinnamon with the burgundy wine. Let come to a boil and simmer for 8-10 minutes. Remove the peaches gently, then strain the hot wine, put back on the heat and continue to boil only the wine. Reduce the wine a third in content. Let cool down. Pour wine into 6 wine glasses, allowing enough room to accommodate the peaches and a tablespoon of whipped cream on top. Serve warm.

Pasquale (Pat) Rocco

BILL OF FARE

RUSSIA

MUTTON SOUP
RUSSIAN SALAD
CHICKEN GREGORIAN
COTTAGE CHEESE MUFFINS
CHESTNUT CREAM

MUTTON SOUP
Russian

1½-pounds mutton
½ cup onions
1½ tablespoons oil
2 tablespoons flour
2 egg yolks

½ teaspoon turmeric
2 tablespoons vinegar
Parsley, chopped
Salt and pepper to taste

Dice meat and place in pot of water, bring to boil and cook about 1½ hours, skimming occasionally. Remove meat from pot and strain stock. Dice onions and fry lightly in oil, add flour and brown. Blend in hot stock, add all meat which has been trimmed and boned, flavor with turmeric, season with salt and pepper and bring to boil. Boil vinegar separately, add to stock and boil again. Shortly before serving, beat egg yolks, add to soup, heat without boiling.

Pasquale (Pat) Rocco
Albany County

RUSSIAN SALAD
Russian

¼ head crisp lettuce, torn into
   bite size pieces
¼-pound pickled tongue, diced

¼-pound ham, diced
¼ cup mayonnaise
Salt and pepper to taste

Combine all ingredients except lettuce and mix well. Fold lettuce into mixture, chill and serve.

Pasquale (Pat) Rocco

CHICKEN GREGORIAN
Russian

4 small chickens
6 garlic cloves
5 tablespoons butter, melted
4 tomatoes
½ cup onion, chopped
⅓ pint Tkemali sauce (made
  with sour plums) or garlic
  sauce

Dill to taste
Parsley to taste
Salt and pepper to taste

Clean, draw and wash chickens. Cut open flat and dry well. Rub well on both sides with garlic, season with salt, pepper and place in a frying pan containing hot butter. Cover with a weighted lid to keep chicken flat. Brown well on both sides. Garnish with parsley, dill and serve the tomatoes, onions and garlic sauce separately.

Garlic Sauce Crush 3-4 cloves of garlic, pour over ⅙ pint hot meat or chicken stock and let stand 2-3 hours.

Pasquale (Pat) Rocco

COTTAGE CHEESE MUFFINS
Russian

1¼-pounds brioche dough
8-ounces cottage cheese, well
  drained
6 tablespoons flour

10 tablespoons or 1 cup plus 2
  tablespoons butter
1 medium egg
Salt and pepper to taste

Line tins with brioche dough. Cream butter and flour together until soft. Add cheese, egg, salt and pepper. Pour mixture into tins and cover with circle of brioche dough, moistening edges to seal. Cover with towel and let stand for 30-35 minutes. Bake in 400 degree oven for 20-25 minutes. Remove from pan and serve.

Pasquale (Pat) Rocco

CHESTNUT CREAM
Russian

1 medium egg yolk
1-ounce sugar
1¾ tablespoons cocoa powder
½ cup milk (warm)
½ cup chestnut purée

2 tablespoons rum flavoring
⅔ pint heavy cream
Chocolate
Water
Sugar

Mix egg yolk, sugar and cocoa powder thoroughly. Whip in warm milk. Cook to a custard and chill. Add rum to chestnut purée and mix with heavy cream. Heat chocolate with water and sugar to a paste. In five glasses, place even amount of chilled chestnut cream. Cover with chocolate and top with custard. Serve.

Pasquale (Pat) Rocco

. . . and Colleagues

BAKED CHICKEN
(IN CREAMED GARLIC AND WINE SAUCE)
Korean

12 pieces chicken, breast and
 legs
¼ fresh garlic, chopped
1 cup white wine
3 small cans cream of
 mushroom soup

2 cans water
2 teaspoons Worcestershire
 sauce
½ teaspoon ginger powder
½ teaspoon black pepper

Mix ingredients and ladle all over chicken parts in covered baking dish. Bake in preheated oven 350 degrees for 1½ hours. Remove cover and brown for another ½ hour. Serve with long grain rice. Ladle wine sauce over rice and serve. Serves 6.

Note: You may add fresh sliced mushrooms.

Sun A. Magner, Executive Chef
Downtown Athletic Club
Albany County

STUFFED WHITE FISH
(IN SHARP CHEESE AND CREAMED WINE SAUCE)
Korean

**6 fresh filets of scrod, haddock
   or sole**

Stuffing:

¼-pound butter, melted
2 cups bread crumbs
2 links of sweet sausage,
   chopped
½ cup fresh mushrooms,
   chopped
2 stalks of scallions, chopped
   (use both green and white
   part)

1 egg
¼ teaspoon ginger powder
¼ teaspoon garlic powder
¼ teaspoon pepper
1 teaspoon parsley flakes, dried
1 teaspoon Worcestershire
   sauce

Mix together in bowl, add water to moisten as desired. Place a rounded tablespoon of stuffing on each filet, and roll with care. Secure with toothpick. Place pats of butter over fish to glaze and bake in covered baking dish 350 degrees for 1 hour, uncover and brown for another 15 minutes.

Wine and cheese Sauce:

¼ cup butter
1 tablespoon garlic, chopped
1 teaspoon Worcestershire
   sauce
3 tablespoons cornstarch

1½ cups water
⅔ cup white wine
½ teaspoon ginger powder
¼ teaspoon salt

Sauté melted butter, with chopped garlic and add rest of ingredients in sauce pan over a low flame. Stir slowly until smooth and hot approximately 5 minutes, then add 1½ cups grated or finely chopped sharp white Cheddar cheese. Stir until cheese melts, then blend together approximately 20 strokes or until sauce thickens. Ladle over fish and green vegetables. Serves 6.

Sun A. Magner, Executive Chef
Downtown Athletic Club
Albany County

CHICKEN MARSALA
Italian

½ cup oil
4 chicken breasts or legs and thighs (or combination of both)
1 cup flour
1 medium onion, chopped

½ pound fresh mushrooms, washed, drained, sliced in half
2 cups Marsala wine
Salt and pepper to taste

Heat oil in fry pan. Coat chicken with flour. Lightly brown in hot oil then set in baking pan (3-inches deep) and set aside. In same fry pan, sauté chopped onions and mushrooms until tender. Add Marsala wine, heat until bubbly. Pour hot wine mixture over chicken in pan, salt and pepper to taste. Cover with aluminum foil. Bake at 400 degrees for 50-55 minutes. Serve hot.

Frank Loperfido, Executive Chef
Onondaga County

MEXICAN MEAT LOAF
Mexican

2½-pounds ground beef
½ medium onion, diced
1 green pepper, diced
1 teaspoon salt
½ teaspoon pepper
½ cup chili sauce
1 teaspoon Worcestershire sauce
1 teaspoon oregano (marjoram)

1 tablespoon beef base (or bouillon)
2 cups bread crumbs
⅔ cup water
5 eggs (save 3 for later use)
¼ cup burgundy wine
1 8-ounce can whole tomatoes (to pour over meat loaf)

Preheat oven to 350 degrees. Combine all ingredients in large bowl. Mold into a half moon shape. Pour 8-ounce can tomatoes over meat loaf. If no whole tomatoes are available, blend 3 of 5 eggs with water well. Rub meat loaf with this mixture until surface appears smooth and well coated.

Richard Cook, Chef
Downtown Athletic Club
Albany County

BOEF A LA WELLINGTON
(Beef Wellington)
French

1 8-ounce filet mignon, peeled	½ teaspoon parsley flakes
2-ounces olive oil	Dry bread crumbs
6-8 medium size mushrooms	Puff pastry (purchase or make)
1 small onion	1 egg
4-ounces butter	Goose liver
8-ounces brandy, (cooking)	1-ounce water
8-ounces sherry, (cooking)	

Peel (take off chain and fat) the filet. Heat the olive oil in a 6-inch sauté pan. Sear the filet in hot oil to a golden brown, reserve. Make a duxelle: grind the mushrooms and onion fine, sauté in the 4-ounces of butter until cooked soft. Add brandy, parsley and sherry wine, cook until reduced to a thick substance. Add enough dry bread crumbs to bind onion, mushrooms and liquids together, and refrigerate to cool. Roll out a purchased 4-inch x 4-inch piece of puff pastry very thin. Beat the egg, apply to all four corners of pastry (enough to seal). Place 2 tablespoons of the duxelle, flattened out, on the filet. Top the duxelle with a very thin slice of goose liver the size of the filet. Place this on the pastry and fold the four corners together, making sure they are sealed. Place folded side down on a metal pie plate. Brush with remaining beaten egg. Add water to pie plate (enough so bottom won't burn). Bake in hot oven at 500 degrees no longer than 20 minutes for medium rare. Serve with a bordelaise sauce. Serves 1.

Jay Porter, Executive Chef
Henry G's Restaurant
Washington County

SALTIMBOCCA
Italian

3 slices Prosciutto ham, sliced paper thin	6-8 mushrooms, sliced
	Mozzarella cheese, sliced
3 tender veal scallopines	1½ ounces Marsala wine
1½ ounces flour	Salt and pepper to taste
1 ounce olive oil	Gravy from veal stock

Place ham slice on veal and pound into veal. Flour veal, keeping ham on scallopine. Sauté in olive oil with mushrooms. Remove meat to platter, cover with Mozzarella cheese slices. Drain grease from pan. Add wine, salt and pepper to mushrooms and make gravy. Pour gravy with mushrooms over veal and heat under broiler until cheese melts. Serves 1.

Joseph Rizzo, Chef
Rizzo's Restaurant
Otsego County

SOUR HOT SOUP WITH SHRIMP
Oriental

4 ounces fresh shrimp, shelled and deveined
2 ounces lean ground pork
4 cups clear chicken broth
3 cups cold water
1 piece ginger root
1 clove garlic, peeled and crushed
3 eggs, beaten with ¼ teaspoon salt, dash black pepper, ½ teaspoon Accent

2 tablespoons oil (for frying shrimp and pork)
2 stalks scallions, chopped
1 teaspoon salt
2 tablespoons soy sauce
2 tablespoons cornstarch
3 tablespoons rice vinegar
½ teaspoon black pepper

Wash the shrimp in cold water and drain well. Wipe away the water with paper towels. Cut shrimp into ¼-inch pieces.

Marinade for Shrimp and ground pork:

¼ teaspoon salt
Dash black pepper

¾ tablespoon soy sauce
1 tablespoon dry sherry wine

In a bowl mix shrimp pieces and ground pork with above ingredients and marinate for about 20 minutes at room temperature. Pour 2 tablespoons oil in a wok or skillet, add ginger and garlic to the hot oil and sizzle for a while. Discard them. Put the shrimp and ground pork mixture into the hot oil and stir fry until they are cooked. Turn out on a plate. Mix 1 teaspoon salt, 2 tablespoons soy sauce and 2 tablespoons cornstarch with 1 cup cold water and set aside. Put 1 piece ginger root in 4 cups clear chicken broth and 2 cups cold water in a saucepan and bring to a boil. Pour the cooked shrimp and pork mixture into the boiling soup and add the 1 cup cold water mixed with salt, soy sauce and cornstarch into the above 6 cups of boiling soup. Turn heat to medium low and pour the beaten eggs very slowly into the soup. Continue stirring the soup while pouring the egg. Then add vinegar, ¼ teaspoon black pepper and scallion into the soup. Let each person add pepper to his own taste. Serve hot.

Note: Mrs. Fong is a well-known Chinese Cooking instructor, soon to publish her own Cookbook. She received her training in Hong Kong before moving to the United States. Mrs. Fong has been demonstrating Chinese cooking since 1974.

Chi Hua L. Fong, Chef
Schenectady County

BLITZ TORTE
German

½ cup butter
½ cup confectioners' sugar
4 eggs, separated
1½ teaspoons vanilla
1 cup flour
1 teaspoon baking powder

3 tablespoons milk
¼ teaspoon cream of tartar
1 cup sugar
1 teaspoon vinegar
1 3-ounce package almonds,
  blanched

Cream together the butter and confectioners' sugar. Beat in yolks and ½ teaspoon vanilla. Sift together flour and baking powder and fold them alternately with the milk into the mixture. Pour into 9-inch pans (greased and floured).

Meringue:
Beat egg whites with cream of tartar until stiff. Gradually add granulated sugar, vinegar and remaining vanilla. Spread over batter filled pans. Sprinkle with almonds. Bake for 25-35 minutes at 325 degrees.

Filling:
1 cup sugar
3 tablespoons flour
1 cup sour cream

4 egg yolks
Dash of salt

Combine all and cook in a double boiler until thick, stirring constantly. Takes 20 to 30 minutes to cook flour thoroughly without boiling mixture. Cool, chill and spread between layers leaving almond topped layer for top.

Hilda Schneider, Chef
Cobble Hill Inn
Essex County

GUACŌMOLE
Mexican

1 ripe avocado
1 teaspoon lemon juice
¼ teaspoon garlic powder
¼ teaspoon salt

¼ cup of green chile salsa
1 tablespoon onion, minced
2 tablespoons tomatoes, diced

Mash avocado and lemon juice. Add garlic powder, salt, chile salsa, minced onions and diced tomatoes. Stir. Serve with freshly fried tostado chips.

Marilyn Farrell, Chef
JUST A FIESTA RESTAURANT
Saratoga County

COUNTY INDEX

American Cancer Society
New York State Division, Inc. 6725 Lyons Street
P.O. Box 7   East Syracuse, NY 13057

Please send me _____ copies of the 1982 I Love New York Cooking
From Other Lands Cookbook for a $6.00 donation per copy (plus $1.00
per copy for postage and handling). Allow 3-5 weeks for delivery.

I enclose an additional donation of $_____.

Enclosed is my check or money order for $_____.
Please make check payable to the American Cancer Society.)

Name_____

Address_____ Zip_____

City_____ State_____ County_____

American Cancer Society
New York State Division, Inc. 6725 Lyons Street
P.O. Box 7   East Syracuse, NY 13057

Please send me _____ copies of the 1982 I Love New York Cooking
From Other Lands Cookbook for a $6.00 donation per copy (plus $1.00
per copy for postage and handling). Allow 3-5 weeks for delivery.

enclose an additional donation of $_____.

Enclosed is my check or money order for $_____.
(Please make check payable to the American Cancer Society.)

Name_____

Address_____ Zip_____

City_____ State_____ County_____

American Cancer Society
New York State Division, Inc. 6725 Lyons Street
P.O. Box 7   East Syracuse, NY 13057

Please send me _____ copies of the 1982 I Love New York Cooking
From Other Lands Cookbook for a $6.00 donation per copy (plus $1.00
per copy for postage and handling). Allow 3-5 weeks for delivery.

enclose an additional donation of $_____.

Enclosed is my check or money order for $_____.
Please make check payable to the American Cancer Society.)

Name_____

Address_____ Zip_____

City_____ State_____ County_____

Re-OrderAdditionalCopies